Graduation
A Time for Change

Other For Better or For Worse® Collections

The Big 5-0
Sunshine and Shadow
Middle Age Spread
Growing Like a Weed
Love Just Screws Everything Up
Starting from Scratch
"There Goes My Baby!"
Things Are Looking Up . . .
What, Me Pregnant?
If This Is a Lecture, How Long Will It Be?
Pushing 40
It's All Downhill from Here
Keep the Home Fries Burning
The Last Straw
Just One More Hug
"It Must Be Nice to Be Little"
Is This "One of Those Days," Daddy?
I've Got the One-More-Washload Blues . . .

Retrospectives

All About April
The Lives Behind the Lines: 20 Years of For Better or For Worse
Remembering Farley: A Tribute to the Life of Our Favorite Cartoon Dog
It's the Thought that Counts . . . Fifteenth Anniversary Collection
A Look Inside . . . For Better or For Worse: The 10th Anniversary Collection

Little Books

Isn't He Beautiful?
Isn't She Beautiful?
Wags and Kisses
A Perfect Christmas

Graduation
A Time for Change

A *For Better or For Worse*® Collection by Lynn Johnston

**Andrews McMeel
Publishing**

Kansas City

www.FBorFW.com

99 00 01 02 03 BAH 10 9 8 7 6 5 4 3 2 1

ISBN: 0-7407-1844-4

Library of Congress Catalog Card Number: 2001088696

WHOA! IT'S HERE, MIKE! IT'S ABOUT THE AWARD WE WERE NOMINATED FOR—IT'S FROM THE ADJUDICATORS!

DID WE WIN? DID WE WIN?!!

"THE JURY IS PLEASED TO INFORM YOU THAT YOUR WORK HAS RECEIVED AN HONORABLE MENTION."

HONORABLE MENTION?!! COULDN'T WE COME IN 3RD OR 4TH OR SOMETHING?

YEAH!... WHAT CAN YOU DO WITH AN HONORABLE MENTION?

WAIT! DON'T THROW THAT LETTER OUT! WE DIDN'T WIN THE LENS AND LETTERS AWARD, BUT HONORABLE MENTION IS GOOD!

HEY, YOU WERE THE ONE WHO SAID IT WAS JUST NICE TO BE NOMINATED!

I WANTED THE AWARD FOR MY DAD, MIKE.

YOUR DAD?!!—HE DOESN'T EVEN LOOK AT YOUR WORK, MAN'!

I KNOW... I THOUGHT MAYBE HE WOULD IF WE WON.

MY DAD STILL WANTS ME TO GO INTO HIS BUSINESS, MIKE. I TOLD HIM I WAS SERIOUS ABOUT BEING A PHOTOGRAPHER.

HE SAID PHOTOGRAPHY WAS A HOBBY, AND IF I WAS SERIOUS, I'D TAKE ACCOUNTING OR MARKETING AND WORK WITH HIM.

IT'S THE OLD "BOTTOM LINE" AGAIN. HE SAYS HE WANTS ME TO HAVE A GOOD LIVING...

... I JUST WANT TO HAVE A GOOD LIFE.

THIS IS A NICE ROOM, WEED. WAS IT YOUR SISTER'S?

NAH...THE ROOMS IN THIS WING ARE JUST FOR GUESTS.

EXCEPT FOR LUCILLE AND THE CARETAKER, THE PLACE IS USUALLY EMPTY. MY PARENTS ARE NEVER HERE.

MOM WANTS TO SELL, BUT DAD REFUSES.

WHY? THIS HOUSE IS FAR TOO BIG FOR TWO PEOPLE!

THAT'S TRUE... BUT YOU DON'T KNOW THE SIZE OF HIS EGO.

MY DAD WAS A REFUGEE. HE BUILT HIS BUSINESS HIMSELF... MADE A FORTUNE... AND, TO HIM, THIS HOUSE IS SORT OF A MONUMENT.

WHEN WE WERE KIDS, MY SISTER AND I COULDN'T IMAGINE HOW PEOPLE LIVED IN TINY APARTMENTS. NOW, WE CAN'T IMAGINE LIVING LIKE THIS.

BUT YOU MUST STILL CALL IT HOME.

KNOW WHAT HOME IS TO ME, MIKE? MY CAR AND MY BACKPACK AND MY CAMERAS. THAT'S ALL I NEED TO BE "HOME."

...I'M SORRY.

EXCUSE ME... I'VE MADE YOU BOYS A SNACK.

LUCILLE, YOU'RE AN ANGEL!

BUT IT'S LATE. YOU USUALLY GO HOME AT 6.

MY FAMILY KNOWS WHERE I AM. BESIDES, I WANTED TO SEE YOU, JO.

THIS LADY RAISED ME, MIKE!

RAISED YOU?!! YOU WERE TOO BUSY RAISING THE DEVIL TO BE RAISED BY ANYBODY!—YOU JUST SORT OF RAISED YOURSELF!

AND EXCEPT FOR THE HAIR AND THOSE AWFUL GLASSES—YOU'RE NOT DOING TOO BAD A JOB OF IT.

MICHAEL! I DIDN'T THINK WE'D FIND YOU IN THIS CROWD!

HI, MOM! DAD!

CAN I TRY ON YOUR HAT?

THEY'RE CALLING ALL THE GRADUANDS—I'D BETTER GO!

EVERYBODY'S HERE, MIKE! UNCLE PHIL, GORD AN' TRACEY, DEANNA AN' LAWRENCE! WE'RE ALL GOING TO WATCH YOU WALK UP ON THE STAGE AN' GET YOUR DIPLOMA!!!

AND YOU'RE WEARING SHORTS?!!!

AND FOR JOURNALISM, WE CONFER THE DEGREE OF BACHELOR OF ARTS, WITH HONORS...

ANGEL PARMINO, MOHAMMAD PATEL...

MICHAEL PATTERSON...

WHONK!!

WEIRD... OUT OF A THOUSAND NOSES IN THIS AUDITORIUM TODAY...

...I KNOW THAT WAS MY DAD'S.

SNF!

CONGRATULATIONS, HONEY! WE'RE SO PROUD OF YOU!

WAY TO GO, MAN!

THANKS, GORDON.

SO, UGLY BROTHER... WHAT'S THE BEST THING ABOUT GRADUATING FROM UNIVERSITY?

IT'S OVER, SIS ...IT'S ALL OVER.

ACTUALLY, MIKE... YOU'VE JUST BEGUN.

HONEY, HAVE YOU SEEN MY GARDENING GLOVES?

I THINK I HUNG THEM UP IN THE GARAGE.

KNOW WHAT I SAW ON TV, MOM?

THIS GUY HUNG SOME GLOVES ON A NAIL LIKE THAT AN' A SPIDER WENT INSIDE ONE OF THE FINGERS.

THEN, WHEN HE PUT HIS GLOVES ON — IT BIT HIM, LIKE **THIS!**

HIS FINGER SWELLED UP SO MUCH, HE HAD TO GO TO THE HOSPITAL!

DID YOUR MOM FIND HER GARDENING GLOVES, APRIL?

UH HUH

AN' SHE'S JUMPING UP AN' DOWN ON THEM!

THAT WAS COOL SEEING MIKE'S GRADUATION!

DADDY, WHY DOES EVERYONE WEAR FLAT HATS?

WELL, IT COMES FROM AN OLD TRADITION, APRIL.

IN THE 18TH CENTURY, SCHOLARS DECIDED THAT IF YOU HAD A DIPLOMA IN ONE HAND AND WERE SHAKING HANDS WITH THE OTHER, YOU SHOULD HAVE A PLACE TO PUT YOUR DRINK.

REALLY?

JOHN, IF YOU DON'T KNOW THE ANSWER TO A QUESTION... YOU SHOULDN'T MAKE ONE UP!

WHY NOT?

...THAT'S HOW I PASSED ENGLISH.

YOU GET TO GRADUATE NEXT, ELIZABETH!

IT'S GRADE 13 GRAD, APRIL, SO IT'S NOT REALLY IMPORTANT.

BUT YOU STILL HAFTA WEAR A GOWN AN' A FUNNY HAT.

IT'S JUST A FORMALITY HERE. IT'S NOT REALLY IMPORTANT.

AND YOU GET A DIPLOMA!

NOT IMPORTANT.

SO WHY DOES EVERYBODY GET DRESSED UP AN' GO OUT FOR A BIG PARTY AFTERWARDS?

THAT PART IS IMPORTANT!

WHAP! WHACK! WHAM! WHAP! WHACK!!

APRIL, WHAT ARE YOU DOING?

I'M NOT APRIL! I'M SOCKHEAD THE SUPERHERO, DEFENDER OF GOOD AN' FIGHTER OF EVIL!

SNIFF? BLEAH!

THESE ARE DISGUSTING!... WHY IN THE WORLD WOULD YOU RUN AROUND WITH A BUNCH OF DIRTY SOCKS?

MOM, THEY WOULDN'T BE WEAPONS IF THEY WERE CLEAN!

NEEEROWWW!! SOCKHEAD THE SUPER HERO HITS WART-SPEED LOOKING FOR ENEMIES.

AH-HAH!...IT'S THE DISGUSTING DIRT-SUCKING VACURON ABOUT TO ATTACK THE PLANET FOOG!!

TAKE THAT AN' THAT AN' THAT AN' THAT AN' THAT!!

MOM, APRIL IS RUNNING AROUND TYING STUFF UP WITH MY OLD SKATING TIGHTS!

SHE'S ALSO GOT ONE OF YOUR KNEE-HIGHS PULLED OVER HER FACE, AN' THAT COULD BE DANGEROUS!

ELIZABETH, SHE'S SAFE, SHE'S HAPPY. LEAVE HER ALONE!

MLLARR BBPP!

BLEAH!... NEVER STICK YOUR TONGUE OUT WHEN YOU'VE GOT A KNEE-HIGH ON YOUR HEAD!

APRIL, WHERE ARE YOU GETTING ALL THOSE OLD SOCKS AN' STUFF FROM? A BOX IN THE LAUNDRY ROOM.

MOM SAID I COULD HAVE THEM TO MAKE SOCKOLIZERS. WHAT'S A SOCKO-LIZER?

WHACK!

IT'S NOT MY FAULT, ELIZABETH... YOU ASKED!!!

20

OK, LIZARDBREATH! YOU ARE NOW THE SWORE NENEMY OF SOCKHEAD THE SUPERHERO!

YOU'LL NEVER GET ME, SOCKHEAD! I CAN RUN FASTER, THINK BETTER AN' I'M STRONGER THAN YOU ARE!

BUT MY WEAPONS ARE SUPERIOR!

THEY'RE SOCKS, BOZO! WHAT MAKES YOU THINK YOURS ARE SUPERIOR?!

BLAPPP!

MINE ARE WET!

WHAP! WHAP! WHAK!

IT'S NICE TO SEE THAT ELIZABETH WILL STILL PLAY WITH APRIL, EL... EVEN THOUGH THERE'S SUCH A BIG AGE DIFFERENCE!

UH-HUH!—AND THE BEST THING ABOUT HAVING A MATURE KID OUT THERE IS...

ALL THOSE OLD SOCKS THEY WERE PLAYING WITH HAVE BEEN PUT AWAY AFTERWARDS!

WHERE ARE YOU GOING, APRIL?

JUST TO THE RAVINE.

YOU'RE NOT GOING DOWN TO THE RIVER, ARE YOU? YOU'RE NOT SUPPOSED TO GO THERE ALONE.

I KNOW.

I JUST LIKE TO COME TO FARLEY'S TREE SOMETIMES.

ME TOO.

AND SOMETIMES I PRETEND HE'S HERE WITH ME.

DO YOU THINK ABOUT FARLEY A LOT, ELIZABETH?

UH-HUH, ESPECIALLY HERE, WHERE HE'S BURIED... OR WHEN I GO DOWN TO THE RIVER.

HE SAVED MY LIFE, DIDN'T HE?

HE SURE DID. GRANDMA CARRIE SAYS HE'S YOUR GUARDIAN ANGEL.

IS THERE REALLY SUCH A THING AS A GUARDIAN ANGEL?

I THINK SO.

SIGH... I WISH THERE WAS A WAY WE COULD KNOW FOR SURE.

I'LL MISS YOU WHEN YOU GO TO UNIVERSITY, ELIZABETH.

I'LL MISS YOU, TOO.

I DON'T LIKE IT WHEN PEOPLE GO AWAY. I GET SCARED SOMETIMES.

SO DO I!

BUT THE TRUTH IS... WHEN SOMEBODY LOVES YOU, THEY ALWAYS COME BACK......

NO MATTER WHAT.

WHERE HAVE YOU TWO BEEN? SUPPER IS ON THE TABLE!

I THOUGHT YOU WEREN'T GONNA COOK TONIGHT, MOM!

WELL, I FELT GUILTY LETTING YOU ALL FORAGE FOR YOURSELVES, SO I WHIPPED UP A LITTLE CASSEROLE.

...OH.

I JUST WANTED A PEANUT BUTTER SANDWICH.

I WAS GONNA HAVE A BOWL OF CEREAL.

AND I WAS LOOKING FORWARD TO A HOT DOG.

TELL ME WHAT PLANET WE'RE ON, CONNIE. I JUST APOLOGIZED TO MY FAMILY FOR MAKING THEM SOMETHING TO EAT.

THIS IS THE BACKPACK I BOUGHT, MICHAEL...IT HOLDS MORE THAN A SUITCASE!

LOOKS GOOD, DEANNA!

WE HAVE A LONG LIST OF STUFF TO BRING... THONGS TO WEAR IN THE SHOWER, STRING, PENS, SCISSORS, TAPE AND LOTS OF CANDLES.

THERE'S NO ELECTRICITY IN THE BUILDING WE'LL BE SLEEPING IN.

SO—YOU'LL BE CAMPING!

YEAH. THEY SAID WE'LL HAVE TO CHECK OUR SHOES EVERY MORNING BECAUSE OF SCORPIONS.

SO...YOU'LL BE CAREFUL.

I AM REALLY LOOKING FORWARD TO THIS TRIP TO HONDURAS. OUR FIRST CLINIC WILL BE SET UP IN OLANCHITO.

IT'S A SMALL VILLAGE IN THE NORTH. PRETTY HARD TO GET TO — EVEN WORSE SINCE THE FLOODING.

WE'LL BE DOING CHECKUPS, GIVING OUT GLASSES, DOING MINOR SURGERY...

SURGERY?!!

UH—HUH

THESE PEOPLE CAN'T GET TO A HOSPITAL—SO WE'RE BRINGING A HOSPITAL TO THEM.

AIRPORT TERMINAL
INTERNATIONAL DEPARTURES

I WON'T BE ABLE TO PHONE YOU FROM OLANCHITO. THEY STILL SEND WIRES BY MORSE CODE!

INTERNATIONAL DEPARTURES
GATES 17-27

BUT I'LL WRITE!

AND KEEP A DIARY. RECORD EVERYTHING!

I WILL. I PROMISE.

EXCUSE ME. I'M KEVIN SMYTHE, ONE OF THE SURGEONS — ARE YOU OUR PHARMACIST?

YES. DEANNA SOBINSKI. I'M PLEASED TO MEET YOU!

GOODBYE, MICHAEL. I LOVE YOU — AND DON'T WORRY ABOUT ME. I'LL BE IN GOOD HANDS.

DEANNA'S GONE, WEED

WELL, THAT'S OVER WITH!

SHE WON'T BE BACK UNTIL CHRISTMAS!

TIME PASSES, MAN—AN' WE'VE GOTTA FOCUS ON WORK! WE HAVE THE IRELAND TRIP COMING UP, BUT RIGHT NOW, WE'RE IN A NON-REV SITUATION!

WEDDING AN' GRAD SHOTS AREN'T GONNA BUY THE GROCERIES—AND THE LAST 2 ARTICLES YOU WROTE JUST BARELY PAID THE RENT!

WOW. I THOUGHT UNIVERSITY WAS TOUGH.

YEAH...THEN YOU FIND OUT THAT THE FINAL EXAM COMES **AFTER** YOU GRADUATE.

SO, THERE'S THE BAD NEWS, MAN.

YOU'RE RIGHT, WEED. THERE'S NO WAY WE CAN MOVE TO TORONTO. NOT 'TIL WE HAVE A RELIABLE CASH FLOW.

I'LL TRY AND GET SOME PART-TIME WORK AT MEGAFOOD. IF I TAKE A NIGHT SHIFT, I CAN WRITE FREELANCE DURING THE DAY.

KNOW WHAT HAPPENED, MIKE? WE LANDED ONE GREAT JOB, HAD SOME GOOD REVIEWS—AN' WE FIGURED WE WERE ON THE ROAD TO SUCCESS.

WE ARE ON THE ROAD TO SUCCESS, MAN!

YEAH... WITH OUR THUMBS OUT!!

WE HAVE TO GIVE YOU A POST-DATED CHEQUE FOR THE RENT, MRS. DINGLE.

WHAT'S THE DIFF? YER LATE AS IT IS, ANYWAY.

I HEAR YOU'LL BE STAYING ON AWHILE.

YEAH!... WE DECIDED NOT TO MOVE TO TORONTO BECAUSE WE KNEW HOW MUCH YOU'D MISS US!

MISS YOU?!! HAH!... I'D MISS YOU LIKE I'D MISS A WART ON MY WAZOO!!!

WHAT'S A WAZOO?

BEATS ME...BUT IF SHE'S GOT ONE, I DON'T WANT TO KNOW ABOUT IT.

26

LOOK, APRIL!—I BOUGHT YOU A REMOTE CONTROL CAR!

SEE HOW IT WORKS? YOU STEER WITH THIS THUMB AND THE OTHER CONTROLS THE SPEED...

NO, NOT LIKE THAT, STEER IT **THIS** WAY!!!

WAIT! YOU'RE NOT DOING IT RIGHT!! LET ME SHOW YOU.

LET'S BACK IT UP AND TURN... OK, LEFT! RIGHT! THIS BABY CAN REALLY FLY!

SEE? THIS IS HOW IT'S DONE!

YOU'RE NOT BORED WITH YOUR NEW TOY ALREADY, ARE YOU, HONEY?

NO...

I HAFTA WAIT UNTIL DAD GETS BORED WITH IT FIRST!

27

HEY, SIS...DEANNA LEFT FOR HONDURAS YESTERDAY. SHE'LL BE GONE 6 MONTHS. ASK ME IF I'M THRILLED. ALSO, THE WEED AND I HAVE VERY LITTLE WORK.

SO, WE'RE ONLY PAYING BILLS WHEN WE HAVE TO. HAVEN'T DONE MY LAUNDRY FOR 3 WEEKS, 'CAUSE GROCERIES COME FIRST. RIGHT NOW, LIFE STINKS...

BUT THIS IS WHAT IT'S ALL ABOUT, MAN—AND I'M MAKING IT ON MY OWN... AND THERE'S NO WAY I'LL TELL MOM AND DAD THAT I'M IN A DEEP FINANCIAL HOLE. NO WAY.

IF **YOU** WANT TO MENTION IT TO THEM, HOWEVER...

MICHAEL'S HAVING MONEY PROBLEMS? BUT I THOUGHT HE HAD A JOB.

YES... BUT IT DOESN'T REALLY START UNTIL AUGUST.

HE HAS FREELANCE WORK, BUT NOT ENOUGH TO PAY THE BILLS.

WELL... I GUESS WE COULD SEND HIM SOMETHING.

JOHN, WE CAN'T KEEP BAILING HIM OUT WHEN HE GETS INTO THESE SITUATIONS. HE HAS TO LEARN HOW TO SURVIVE ON HIS OWN! HE HAS TO LEARN HOW TO **BUDGET**!

IS $200 TOO MUCH?

...BETTER MAKE IT 3.

WE ONLY SEND MICHAEL MONEY WHEN HE'S REALLY IN TROUBLE, EL—AND HE DOESN'T ASK VERY OFTEN.

YOU CAN'T JUST "GET A JOB" THESE DAYS. IT'S TOUGHER THAN IT WAS WHEN WE WERE KIDS—AND EVERY-THING COSTS MORE, TOO.

WELL, I DON'T WANT TO SPOIL HIM, JOHN. BESIDES, EVERY TIME YOU TURN ON THE TUBE, SOMEONE'S TELLING US TO INVEST IN SOMETHING THAT WILL HELP TO SUPPORT US IN OUR OLD AGE!

AND I BELIEVE WE ARE.

JOHN AND I HAVE A GREAT RELATIONSHIP, CONNIE. THE ONLY THING WE DISAGREE ABOUT IS HOW WE DISCIPLINE THE KIDS.

I THINK HE'S TOO EASY ON THEM. HE'S ESPECIALLY LENIENT WITH MICHAEL. HEAVEN ONLY KNOWS WHERE THAT BOY'S MONEY GOES, BUT HERE WE ARE... SENDING HIM ANOTHER CHEQUE!

SO I CALLED MICHAEL AND I TOLD HIM, "YOU'VE GOT TO LEARN HOW TO **SAVE!** — YOU'VE GOT TO LEARN HOW TO **BUDGET!!**"

AND?

HE SAID HE WOULD... AS SOON AS HE HAD SOME MONEY.

WHAT IS IT WITH KIDS, CONNIE? YOU GIVE THEM ADVICE AND THEY DON'T TAKE IT. YOU GIVE THEM RULES AND THEY WANT TO BREAK THEM...

YOU TRY TO PROTECT THEM AND THEY DISAPPEAR! LIZ IS NEVER HOME — I'M GLAD SHE HAS A JOB NOW BECAUSE AT LEAST I KNOW WHERE SHE **IS!!!**

APRIL RIDES HER BIKE SO FAST, I CAN'T WATCH! SHE SEES STUFF ON TV AND THE NET THAT WOULD HAVE BEEN CENSORED WHEN I WAS HER AGE!

SO, AS A PARENT, WHAT CAN YOU DO? YOUR BEST, EL... ALL YOU CAN DO IS YOUR BEST.

FEAR NOT, UGLY BROTHER... SALVATION IS AT HAND! — POP IS SENDING YOU SOME ACTUAL CASH BUCKS, SO FIRE UP YOUR CHEQUEBOOK AND PREPARE TO PAY BILLS!

TICK TAP

BY THE WAY, I'M WORKING FULL TIME AT MEGA-FOOD FOR THE SUMMER. THE MANAGER SAID I WAS HIRED BECAUSE THEY LIKED YOU AND FIGURED THAT IF WE WERE FROM THE SAME FAMILY, I'D BE A GOOD RISK.

THANKS! — IT'S NICE TO KNOW YOU'RE ONLY A DORK WHEN YOU'RE AT HOME!

ARE YOU GOING TO WORK, ELIZABETH?

UH-HUH. EVERYONE AT MEGA-FOOD HAS TO WEAR BLACK PANTS AND WHITE SHIRTS.

THEN WE WEAR GREEN APRONS AND WE EACH HAVE A NAME TAG.

THEY MAKE YOU A NAME TAG?!!

WE HAVE TO KEEP OUR HAIR NEAT AND OFF OUR FACES, AND WE HAVE TO KEEP OUR HANDS CLEAN AT ALL TIMES.

OH.

...TOO BAD—IT WAS STARTING TO SOUND LIKE A COOL JOB!

I'M SO NERVOUS. LAST YEAR I STOCKED SHELVES. THIS IS MY FIRST TIME ON CASH...UN-SUPERVISED!

REMEMBER TO WEIGH STUFF, REMEMBER NAMES OF WEIRD VEGETABLES, REMEMBER TO CHECK BASKETS AND TAG LARGE ITEMS.

REMEMBER TO PUT HEAVY STUFF ON THE BOTTOM, RE-MEMBER TO DOUBLE-BAG CHICKENS, REMEMBER TO WIPE SCANNER, REMEMBER TO...

HEY!

...DON'T FORGET TO SMILE.

THIS CAN HAS A DENT IN IT AND ONE OF THESE EGGS LOOKS "ODD."

NO PROBLEM. WE'LL EXCHANGE THEM.

THIS ASPARAGUS LOOKS A LITTLE DRY. I'VE DECIDED NOT TO TAKE IT.

WE'LL REFUND YOUR MONEY.

YOU DON'T HAVE VITO-BUDS OR NUTRIGRITS. THERE'S NOT ENOUGH VARIETY IN YOUR CEREAL SECTION.

I'LL TELL THE MAN-AGER.

WEIRD. THE MORE PEOPLE HAVE TO EAT...THE MORE THEY COMPLAIN ABOUT IT.

EVER SINCE I STARTED WORKING AT MEGAFOOD, ALL I THINK ABOUT IS GROCERIES!!

I CAN'T LOOK AT A BAG OF FRUIT, A PACKAGE OF MEAT OR A VEGETABLE WITHOUT CALCULATING THE WEIGHT AND THE PRICE!

FOOD! I CAN'T GET IT OUT OF MY MIND. WHEN I SHUT MY EYES, ALL I CAN SEE IS GROCERIES AND PRODUCE AND FOOD!

SUPPER'S READY, HONEY!

...I'M, UH...NOT TOO HUNGRY.

IF YER HAPPY AND ♪ YOU KNOW IT AN' YOU REALLY WANNA SHOW IT, IF YER HAPPY AN' YOU KNOW IT...

WHAT'S THE MATTER WITH EVERYONE?

WE'RE TIRED, APRIL. WE'VE BEEN WORKING ALL DAY.

TSK WELL, WHAT DO YOU THINK I'VE BEEN DOING?!!

THERE YOU ARE, EL! I HAVEN'T SEEN ANYONE AROUND YOUR PLACE FOR THE LAST FEW DAYS!

I KNOW.

LIZ IS ON SHIFT AT MEGA-FOOD, JOHN'S GOING CRAZY AT THE CLINIC, SO I SAID I'D WORK FULL TIME AT THE BOOKSTORE THIS MONTH.

FULL TIME? BUT, ELLY— THE SUMMER IS SO SHORT! WHY ARE YOU SPENDING ALL YOUR TIME INDOORS?

...SO WE CAN AFFORD TO GO SOMEWHERE WARM IN FEBRUARY!

HEY, GORD! I WAS JUST PASSING THROUGH ON MY WAY HOME.

MIKE! IT'S GREAT TO SEE YOU!

I'VE GOT ELIZABETH'S BOY-FRIEND WORKING HERE, AND HE'S REDONE MY ENTIRE ACCOUNTING SYSTEM!—THE KID'S A WIZ!

LOOK AT THIS. HE'S GOT MY BUSINESS ORGANIZED—AND WE'RE ON THE WEB! CHECK IT OUT—PARTS, SERVICE, SALES, EVERYTHING!—ISN'T IT AMAZING?!!

YEAH!

...ANTHONY IS STILL ELIZABETH'S BOYFRIEND?!

HEY, ANTHONY!—GOOD JOB YOU'RE DOING FOR GORD HERE!

THANKS, MIKE.

ROAD SAFETY BEGINS WITH THE GRABBER

ORIGINALLY, I WAS HIRED TO, YOU KNOW, PUMP GAS... BUT WHEN I SAW HOW HE WAS DOING HIS ACCOUNTS AN' STUFF, I FIGURED I COULD, LIKE, HELP HIM OUT!

I WENT TO THE HDD, CREATED A TEMP FOLDER, UPLOADED AND INSTALLED A 2 MEG PATCH. THEN I CONVERTED ALL HIS FILES FROM DOS TO WINDOWS, BUILT A DATABASE, BUZZED UP SOME INPUT FORMS AND QUERY TABLES AND... GENTLEMEN, WE ARE IN PHAT CITY!!!

WHO'S PUMPING GAS?

...I AM.

SO, HOW'S THE FAMILY?

ROSIE'S GETTING BIG! SHE SITS UP NOW AND SMILES ALL THE TIME!

Cola 75¢
ICE COLD
WE RECYCLE

SHE'S A REAL BEAUTY!

AND PAUL?

HE'S 3 NOW! HE LOVES BOOKS AND GAMES... TRACEY HAS HIM IN SWIMMING LESSONS.

IT SURE CHANGES YOU, MIKE. NOTHING MAKES YOU MORE FOCUSED, MORE SENSI-TIVE, MORE MATURE THAN BEING A PARENT.

HEY... I AM SO PROUD OF YOU, MAN.

SO MUCH FOR A NIGHT ON THE TOWN WITH MY OL' BUDDY GORD.

I SEE THE LITTLE BLUE CAR IS HOLDING UP, MIKE.

YOU SOLD US A GOOD ONE, GORDO!

I THOUGHT YOUR SISTER WAS DRIVING IT.

WELL, THE FOLKS DECIDED I NEEDED IT MORE THAN SHE DID.

BUT I'M TAKING IT HOME. FAIR IS FAIR, AND IT'S TIME SHE GOT A CHANCE TO DRIVE IT.

BROKE, HUH?

ROCK BOTTOM.

USED CAR SALES SERVICE

HERE ARE THE KEYS TO THE LITTLE CAR, SIS. NOW THAT YOU HAVE A STEADY JOB, YOU CAN AFFORD TO DRIVE HER.

THANKS, MICHAEL.

SEEMS WEIRD BEING BACK AT THE MALL. I WORKED HERE FOR SO MANY SUMMERS.

THE GUYS AT MEGA-FOOD MISS YOU!

HERE I AM, BACK AT SQUARE ONE. MY CAREER IS STALLED, MY GIRLFRIEND IS IN HONDURAS, MY FRIENDS ARE EITHER MARRIED OR ESTABLISHED SOMEWHERE...

AND I'VE KIND OF LOST MY SENSE OF DIRECTION.

...LET'S GO HOME.

HI, MOM! MIKE PICKED ME UP AFTER WORK! — WE JUST DROVE HOME TOGETHER.

WHERE IS HE?

AS SOON AS HE SAW THE HOUSE, HE SAID HE FELT NOSTALGIC AND WANTED TO GO INSIDE.

APPARENTLY THERE'S ONE SPECIAL PLACE WHERE HE LIKES TO GO ALONE.

PIZZA

So, life outside university isn't quite what you thought it would be.

I'm not getting much work, pop.

I write freelance for 2 magazines and for the Valley Voice, I help out on a website, but I need something steady.

Your trip to Ireland is coming up soon. It's a job that could launch your career!

Well... I'm not counting on anything.

You can count on your fingers, Mike... it's amazing what you can accomplish with your own two hands.

Hi, Mrs P! I've got the azaleas you ordered. I'll just put them in the back.

Thanks, hon!

Michael! Good to see you, man—it's been ages.

Hey, Lawrence!—I hear you're managing Lakeshore Landscaping!

Yeah, well, I thought I'd be more into botanical research, but this came along and I just "went with the flow."

And how about you?

I'm still swimming upstream.

Something bothering you, Mike? You seem kind of down.

Yeah, well... it's a bit of everything!

Work is slow and my girlfriend is in Honduras with a medical team... she won't be home 'til Christmas.

Really!

My mom did that! She was in Ecuador for a long time. She learned a lot, had some adventures, brought back some souvenirs...

...one of them was ME.

LAWRENCE, YOU WEREN'T BORN IN ECUADOR!

NO, I WAS BORN IN CANADA! MY MOM MET MY FATHER WHILE SHE WAS WORKING IN ECUADOR.

HE WAS A DOCTOR. STILL IS. HE LIVES IN BRAZIL SOMEWHERE. HIS NAME IS PABLO DA SILVA. HE SPECIALIZES IN TROPICAL DISEASES, OR SOMETHING.

WHEN MOM LEFT ECUADOR, SHE WAS EXPECTING ME. MY FATHER PROMISED TO MEET HER HERE AND MARRY HER.

WHAT HAPPENED?

I DUNNO... BUT BY MY WATCH, HE'S A LITTLE LATE.

MOM TOLD ME THAT YOUR DAD WAS BRAZILIAN, LAWRENCE... BUT SHE DIDN'T TELL ME THE REST OF THE STORY.

HE'S MY BIOLOGICAL FATHER. I HAVE NO "DAD."

IT'S STRANGE THAT HE'S NEVER CONTACTED YOU.

I'VE SEEN PICTURES. HE'S TALL. VERY DARK. NOT BAD LOOKING, I GUESS.

MOM SAYS I HAVE HIS HAIR, HIS FACE, HIS SMILE.

AREN'T YOU CURIOUS? WOULDN'T YOU **LIKE** TO MEET HIM?

YES, BUT WHAT'S THE POINT?

...THE THINGS I WANT TO ASK HIM, HE COULD NEVER ADEQUATELY ANSWER.

SO... YOUR MOM, CONNIE, WENT TO ECUADOR WITH A MEDICAL TEAM AND FELL IN LOVE WITH A BRAZILIAN DOCTOR...

WHO WAS MY FATHER.

EVEN THOUGH HE WAS A CAD, SHE'LL TELL YOU THAT IT'S RATHER A ROMANTIC STORY!

LAWRENCE, AS WE SPEAK, MY GIRLFRIEND IS IN HONDURAS, WORKING WITH A MEDICAL TEAM!

WELL, THAT DOESN'T MEAN SHE'S GOING TO RUN AWAY ON YOU, MIKE!

I KNOW... BUT MY IMAGINATION MIGHT!

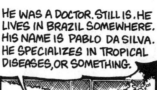

I'VE KNOWN ABOUT LAWRENCE'S FATHER FOR A LONG TIME, MIKE. SINCE I WAS 8.

THE WHOLE STORY?

YES.

CONNIE TOLD MOM EVERYTHING. THEY WERE SITTING AT THE KITCHEN TABLE, HAVING ONE OF THEIR LONG CONVERSATIONS.

LAWRENCE IS MY FRIEND, SIS! IF YOU KNEW, WHY DIDN'T MOM TELL ME?!

WELL, I WASN'T EXACTLY AT THE TABLE...

...I WAS UNDER IT!

WHERE ARE YOU GOING?

TO TALK TO LAWRENCE'S MOM!

I'D LIKE TO WRITE ABOUT SOME OF HER EXPERIENCES IN ECUADOR!

PEOPLE HAVE AMAZING LIVES, ELIZABETH! THERE ARE SO MANY FASCINATING STORIES. —ALL YOU HAVE TO DO IS ASK PEOPLE TO TELL YOU ABOUT THEM!

ARF!

HOW COME HE NEVER ASKS ME?!!

YES, I MET PABLO DA SILVA IN ECUADOR, MICHAEL. WE WERE WITH A TRAVELLING MEDICAL TEAM.

WE WORKED IN SHEDS AND SCHOOLHOUSES WITH NO ELECTRICITY, NO RUNNING WATER, NO SANITATION— AND VERY FEW SUPPLIES.

OUR EQUIPMENT WAS PRIMITIVE. WE WORKED LONG, HARD HOURS. IT WAS EXHAUSTING AND AT TIMES, IT WAS EXTREMELY DIFFICULT.

...AND I LOVED EVERY MINUTE OF IT.

I WAS AN X-RAY TECHNICIAN WITH NO EXPERIENCE. OUR EQUIPMENT ONLY WORKED WHEN WE COULD GET THE GENERATORS TO RUN.

PEOPLE CAME ON FOOT THROUGH THE MOUNTAINS CARRYING THE SICK, CHILDREN CARRYING CHILDREN. FEW OF THEM HAD SHOES.

THEY WOULD LINE UP AT OUR MAKESHIFT CLINICS AND WAIT ALL DAY. SOME WE COULD HELP. OTHERS, WE COULD NOT.

STILL, THEY SMILED AND THEY THANKED US... AND WE LEARNED TO ACCEPT THEIR GRATITUDE AS ONE WOULD ACCEPT A GIFT.

LYNN

MY GIRLFRIEND, DEANNA, IS IN HONDURAS WITH A MEDICAL TEAM, CONNIE. SHE'S THEIR PHARMACIST.

SHE'LL BE BUSY.

IT'S ANOTHER WORLD DOWN THERE, HON... WHEN SHE COMES BACK TO YOU, SHE'LL BE A DIFFERENT PERSON.

TRAVELLING TO PLACES LIKE THIS DEFINITELY CHANGES YOU, MICHAEL.

HOW?

ALWAYS FOR THE BETTER.

LYNN

YOU INTERVIEWED MY MOTHER?

I HATE TO PASS UP A GOOD STORY, LAW-RENCE!

DID YOU KNOW THAT SHE KEEPS TRACK OF YOUR FATHER THROUGH FRIENDS?

I GUESS.

HE'S A PROFESSOR NOW. YOU KNOW HE'S FAMOUS.

MICHAEL, I DON'T CARE WHAT HE'S DOING OR HOW HE'S DOING OR WHERE HE'S DOING IT.

...HE'LL BE LECTURING HERE IN OCTOBER.

LYNN

LOOK AT YOUR PARENTS, LIZ!

I WAS JUST THINKING HOW NICE IT IS TO SEE TWO PEOPLE WHO'VE LIVED TOGETHER FOR OVER 25 YEARS HAVING SO MUCH FUN TOGETHER!

WHAT'S WRONG?

... I WAS JUST THINKING HOW EMBARRASSED I WAS.

WHATCHA LOOKING FOR?

DAD'S LONG UNDER-WEAR. THEY SAY IT GETS COLD IN IRELAND.

OH, NO. I THOUGHT HE HAD THE TWO-PIECE KIND! I DON'T WANNA WEAR THESE!

WHAT'S THIS THING FOR?

I'LL SHOW YOU.

MICHAEL... I DON'T BELIEVE THIS IS A WINDOW!

WELL, I'M ON MY WAY! LIZ IS GONNA DRIVE ME TO THE BUS. AND TOMORROW, WEED AN' I LEAVE FOR IRELAND!

ARE YOU SURE YOU HAVE EVERYTHING?

MOM— YOU'VE ASKED ME THAT QUESTION ABOUT 10 TIMES NOW! YES! I'M SURE. I HAVE ABSO-LUTELY EVERY-THING!!

WHAT'S THIS?

CHEESE!— I THOUGHT YOU MIGHT LIKE A LITTLE NIBBLE ON THE WAY!

SNIFFF?

THAT REMINDS ME...

I NEED SOCKS.

THIS IS IT, WEED— WE'RE FINALLY EN ROUTE!

I EVEN WORE GREEN FOR THE OCCASION!

WE TAKE THE TRAIN FROM DUBLIN TO MULLINGAR. THE O'CONNORS WILL MEET US THERE.

AND THE WORK BEGINS.

HERE'S TO OUR FIRST BIG TIME FREELANCE GIG!

MAY WE SUCCEED BEYOND OUR WILDEST DREAMS!

YOU'RE HAVING WILD DREAMS, MIKE?

ACTUALLY... I HAVEN'T SLEPT MUCH SINCE WE SIGNED THE CONTRACT!

WANNA GO OUT TONIGHT, DAWN? MIKE LEFT ME THE LITTLE BLUE CAR. ... OH ... MAYBE ANOTHER NIGHT THEN.

SHAWNA-MARIE! WHAT'S HAPPENING? NO ... I UNDERSTAND. SURE. I'LL SEE YOU LATER.

I'LL GO OUT WITH YOU, LIZ!

APRIL, I WANT TO GO OUT WITH PEOPLE MY OWN AGE. I'M SORRY, OK?

HMPH! SHE'LL GO OUT WITH HER DUMB FRIENDS... BUT SHE WON'T GO OUT WITH A **SUPER-HERO!**

WHAT'S WITH THE TOWEL, APRIL?

IT'S A CAPE, MRS. POIRIER. ALL SUPERHEROES WEAR CAPES!

I'M SOCKHEAD, THE SUPERHERO... DEFENDER OF GOOD, DESTROYER OF EVIL!

WHAT SUPER POWERS DO YOU HAVE?

FIRST OFF, I CAN FLY. I ALSO HAVE MY DEADLY SOCKOLIZER WEAPONS AN' I CAN CHANGE MY FACE SO NOBODY KNOWS ME!

SO WHAT HAVE YOU SAVED LATELY?

I SAVED THIS!

BUT... THAT'S A CANDY BAR!

I KNOW... I SAVED IT FROM MY SISTER!

SO, MICHAEL'S GONE ON ASSIGNMENT!

UH HUH... HE CALLED FROM DUBLIN YESTERDAY.

HE INTERVIEWED ME THE OTHER DAY, ELLY.

I KNOW. YOU'VE HAD A FEW ADVENTURES IN YOUR LIFE!

HE THINKS YOU SHOULD WRITE YOUR MEMOIRS, CONNIE.

PEOPLE WRITE MEMOIRS WHEN THEY'RE OLD AND GREY. YOU **ARE** OLD AND GREY!

I KNOW... BUT I'M STILL ABLE TO HIDE IT.

44

MUNCH, GRUNCH, MFF, CRUNCH...

SLURRUPPPPP

WE SHOULD THROW OUT SOME OF THE OLD CEREAL, LIZ.

YEAH? HOW COME?

THE RAISIN YOU JUST ATE HAD LEGS ON IT.

CAN'T CATCH ME! CAN'T CATCH ME!

SHRIEK!

HA HA

THAT'S ENOUGH, APRIL I CAN'T PLAY ANY MORE. I'M EXHAUSTED!

ELIZABETH...YOU'RE NOT GETTING OLD, ARE YOU?

SO, WE'VE ALL BEEN ACCEPTED BY DIFFERENT UNIVERSITIES!

THAT APPEARS TO BE THE CASE.

I'M GOING TO BROCK!

I'LL BE IN OTTAWA.

I'M GOING TO WESTERN, LIZ. LIKE YOUR BROTHER.

WOW.

I'M GOING TO NIPISSING. IT'S SORT OF UP NORTH.

UP NORTH?!!-LIZ, IT'S OFF THE MAP!

IT'S JUST AN HOUR BY PLANE, ANTHONY...

BUT IT MUST TAKE FOREVER TO DRIVE THERE!

JUST THINK OF IT AS 3 CDS AND A GOOD CONVERSATION.

HERE ARE SOME PHOTOS WE TOOK OF THE CAMPUS —PRETTY, ISN'T IT.

BUT WHY NIPISSING UNIVERSITY? WHY ARE YOU GOING SO FAR AWAY?

I WANTED TO GO TO A SMALL SCHOOL, ANTHONY.

I GUESS IT HAD TO HAPPEN... DIDN'T IT?

SAYING GOODBYE, I MEAN. WE'VE GOT A COUPLE OF WEEKS LEFT. IT'S NOT LIKE WE HAVE TO SAY GOODBYE THIS MINUTE.

I KNOW...

BUT WE COULD START PREPARING!

WHATCHA DOIN', ELIZABETH?

GOING THROUGH ALL MY STUFF SO I KNOW WHAT TO PACK!

I'VE GOTTA DECIDE WHICH CLOTHES TO TAKE AN' OTHER THINGS, LIKE MY SKIS, MY CDS, MY CLOCK, LAMP, SEWING KIT...

ARE YOU GONNA TAKE YOUR OLD CLOTH BUNNY?

SURE! I HAVE TO TAKE MY CLOTH BUNNY!

THEN YOU REALLY ARE LEAVING, AREN'T YOU?

APRIL, WHAT'S THE MATTER?

ELIZABETH IS PACKING AND SHE'S GOING TO GO AWAY.

I KNOW. SHE'LL BE IN A NEW SCHOOL IN A NEW TOWN— BUT WE'LL VISIT AND WE'LL SEE HER ON HOLIDAYS AND WE'LL WRITE!

I DON'T WANT HER TO GO!!

PEOPLE GROW UP, HONEY, AND THEY START LIVES OF THEIR OWN! SOME DAY YOU'LL GO AWAY, TOO.

THEN I'LL TRY AN' GROW UP AS SLOWLY AS POSSIBLE.

SCRATCH SCRITCH SCRATCH SCRITCH SKRFF SKRATCH

FOR HEAVEN'S SAKE, EDGAR, CUT THAT OUT! — YOU'RE GOING TO DRIVE ME CRAZY!

SCRATCH SCRATCH SCRATCH

SCRATCH, SCRITCH SKRAATCHH SCRATCH SKRITT SCRATCH SKRITT SKRUFF

WEIRD. WHAT?

DAD'S DOWN ON ALL-FOURS, SCRATCHING THE DOG.

MOM, THERE'S AN E-MAIL FROM MICHAEL — IT'S FROM IRELAND!!

WE'RE STAYING IN A SMALL B&B IN BALLYMAHON. TO-MORROW, WE'LL RESEARCH MORE OF THE O'CONNOR FAMILY HISTORY THROUGH THE CHURCH ARCHIVES.

I HAVE NEVER SEEN SUCH ANCIENT BUILDINGS! CASTLES AND BRIDGES, HOUSES AND WALLS ALL MADE OF STONE.

FOR WEED AND MYSELF, THE DAYS FLY BY FAR TOO QUICKLY... WHILE ALL AROUND US... TIME STANDS STILL.

WE FOUND THE ORIGINAL O'CONNOR HOMESTEAD, BUT THE HOUSE WAS DESTROYED LONG AGO.

WE WENT TO THE PLACE WHERE COLM O'CONNOR, HIS MOTHER AND SISTER BOARDED THE COFFIN SHIP AND SAILED FOR CANADA.

WE'VE TRACED THE FAMILY BACK 5 GENERATIONS — AND IT'S BEEN AN INTER-ESTING EXERCISE. PEOPLE HERE KEEP MENTAL RECORDS.

YOU JUST HAVE TO KNOW HOW TO RETRIEVE THEM.

WILL MICHAEL BE HOME SOON?

THIS WEEK!

HE HAS TO GET HERE BEFORE I LEAVE!

I WANT TO SAY GOODBYE. I ALSO WANT TO ASK HIM STUFF ABOUT UNIVERSITY— LIKE WHAT HAPPENS DURING FROSH WEEK AN' WHAT'S IT LIKE LIVING IN REZ!

I CAN TELL YOU ALL ABOUT THAT STUFF, LIZ! NOTHING'S CHANGED MUCH SINCE I WENT TO SCHOOL.

I LOVE YOU, DAD... BUT I REALLY WANT TO BELIEVE THAT IT **HAS!**

SO... YOU'RE ALL PACKED, I SEE.

YES. DAD WANTS ME TO TAKE THE TRAIN TO NORTH BAY.

I'M LEAVING FOR LONDON TODAY. I'M GOING TO MISS YOU, LIZ— I CAME TO ASK YOU IF...

ANTHONY— LET'S NOT COMPLICATE OUR LIVES BY MAKING PROMISES.

WE'VE BEEN MORE THAN FRIENDS FOR A LONG TIME. NOTHING IS EVER GOING TO CHANGE THAT. JUST KEEP IN TOUCH... OK?

OK

I PROMISE.

THANK YOU, GENTLEMEN. WE'LL SEE YOU IN 2 WEEKS.

IT WAS A PLEASURE, MR. O'CONNOR.

IN THE PAST FEW DAYS, I HAVE WALKED FAR-THER, ASKED MORE QUESTIONS AND WRITTEN MORE THAN I HAVE IN MY ENTIRE LIFE!

WHEN THEY SAID IT WERE A "JOB," ME SON... THEY WAS RIGHT! NOW WE JUST HAVE TO TURN OUT A GOOD STORY!

I CAN SEE WHY THE FOLKS WHO LEAVE IRE-LAND MISS HER SO. SHE GETS INTO YOUR BLOOD, SHE BECOMES PART OF YOU. SHE TOUCHES YOUR SOUL.

YES, INDEED.

...I WISH THEY HAD PUBS LIKE THAT IN CANADA.

MOM, WHY DO I HAFTA WEAR THIS FRILLY THING?

WE'RE GOING TO A FANCY OUTDOOR PARTY, APRIL, AND WE'RE ALL DRESSING UP!

CAN I WAIT FOR YOU OUTSIDE?

YES, BUT REMEMBER...

I DON'T WANT **ANYTHING** TO HAPPEN TO THAT DRESS !!!

Row 1

WE'RE MEETING MICHAEL AT THE AIRPORT FIRST, AN' THEN WE'RE GOING TO THE TRAIN STATION TO SAY GOODBYE TO ELIZABETH?

UH-HUH

ELIZABETH PATTERSON NORTH BAY

WE DIDN'T EXPECT ALL THIS EXCITEMENT IN ONE DAY, BUT THAT'S LIFE!

LOOK AT ALL THE BAGS AND BOXES! WE'LL HAVE TO CHECK THESE AT THE TRAIN BEFORE WE GO TO THE AIRPORT!

I'M SORRY, MOM—I DIDN'T THINK MOVING WOULD BE SO MUCH WORK!

DON'T WORRY, HONEY. I DON'T MIND THE CHAOS!

ELIZABETH PATTERSON NORTH BAY

...IT KEEPS ME FROM CRYING.

Row 2

LOOK AT THIS, MIKE—WE HAVE A WELCOMING COMMITTEE!

ARRIVALS

HEY, BIG BROTHER, YOU'RE JUST IN TIME TO SAY GOODBYE TO ME. IN 3 HOURS I'LL BE ON THE TRAIN TO NORTH BAY!

HOW WAS IRELAND?

DID YOU GET A GOOD STORY?

OH, MAN, WE'VE GOT SO MUCH TO TELL YOU!

* CANADIAN CUSTOMS

SOME DAY, WHEN I'M BIG, I'M GOING TO REMEMBER TO TALK TO SHORT PEOPLE.

Row 3

I'D LIKE TO SPEND MORE TIME WITH YOUR FAMILY, MIKE, BUT I HAVE TO GET HOME.

HONEY, WE KNOW YOU'RE TIRED. MAYBE YOU SHOULD GO WITH JOSEF.

ARE YOU KIDDING? I WANT TO SEE LIZARD-BREATH TAKE OFF FOR UNIVERSITY!

I WANT TO SEE MY LITTLE SISTER STEP INTO THE REAL WORLD!

TRACK 2

THE FIRST STEP SEEMS LIKE SUCH A BIG ONE!

N R

'BYE, LIZ! | TAKE CARE. | CALL WHEN YOU GET THERE. | WE LOVE YOU!

ALL ABOAARD!!

AAAHHH...FREEDOM! I'M FREE, FREE, FREE, FREE, FREE!

DEAR STUDENT,... YOU WILL NEED $500 FOR BOOKS, RESIDENCE DAMAGE DEPOSIT $175, FROSH KIT $50, BUS PASS AND STUDENT CARD $100... ACTIVITIES CLUBS, $ PARKING $

AN' THAT'LL BE $6.75 FOR THE SANDWICH AN' SODA.

SNAK SERVER

I'M GLAD YOU CAME WITH US TO SEE ELIZABETH OFF, MICHAEL. | ME, TOO

I'LL SEND YOU MY STORY AS I WRITE IT! | GOOD LUCK!

SO, IT'S JUST THE 3 OF US NOW. IT'S GOING TO BE KIND OF FUN HAVING THE WHOLE HOUSE TO OURSELVES, ISN'T IT, APRIL?

APRIL?

WHEN THEY LIVED HERE, MIKE AND ELIZABETH WERE HARDLY EVER HOME.

WHEN THEY WERE HERE, THEY WERE EITHER TALKING ON THE PHONE OR DIGGING IN THE FRIDGE. THEY LEFT LAUNDRY ON THE FLOOR AND DISHES IN THE SINK.

THEIR ROOMS WERE A MESS. THEIR MUSIC WAS LOUD. THE WAY THEY DRESSED DROVE ME CRAZY.

AND NOW THEY'RE GONE. THE PLACE IS QUIET AND TIDY. I MISS THEM. AND I'M WONDERING...

MAYBE, IF I'D BEEN A LITTLE MORE TOLERANT, IT WOULD FEEL LIKE WE'D HAD A LITTLE MORE TIME.

53

IS ELIZABETH AT UNIVERSITY NOW, MOM?

UH-HUH. SHE'LL BE GOING THROUGH ORIENTATION.

WHAT DOES THAT MEAN?

WELL, YOU TOUR THE CAMPUS AND THE TOWN, YOU MEET OTHER STUDENTS AND SOME OF THE STAFF.

YOU GET YOUR COURSES ORGANIZED, BUY YOUR BOOKS AND SETTLE INTO YOUR ROOM.

AND THEN WHAT HAPPENS?

DIS ORIENTATION!

THERE. I'M TOTALLY UNPACKED.—I CAN'T BELIEVE I'M ACTUALLY LIVING IN RESIDENCE AT NIPISSING U!

IT'S LIKE HAVING MY OWN APARTMENT!...WELL, SORT OF!

I'VE BOUGHT SOME GROCERIES AND ORGANIZED THE KITCHEN—BUT THE GIRL WHO'S SHARING WITH ME STILL HASN'T SHOWN UP!

...I HOPE IT'S SOMEONE I'LL LIKE!

CANDACE?!! ELIZABETH!

THIS HAS TO BE RIGHT. MY KEY IS FOR THIS BUILDING.

THEN, YOU'RE MY ROOMMATE?

MAN! OF ALL THE PEOPLE IN THE WORLD, I NEVER EXPECTED TO MEET YOU HERE!

HEY—YOU GOTTA SHARE YOUR SPACE WITH SOMEONE!

AN' IF WE LIKE EACH OTHER, IT'S COOL ... IF WE DON'T, IT'S KARMA!

CANDACE? WHY DID YOU CHOOSE NIPISSING UNIVERSITY?

MY MOM'S SISTER LIVES IN TOWN. SHE'S NUTS BUT OK...

MIND IF I SMOKE, LIZ?

UH, I GUESS...

NOT AS LONG AS I'M IN MY CELL, RIGHT?

YEAH...MY MOM WANTED ME TO GO WHERE THERE WAS FAMILY.—LIKE I'M GONNA GO LOOKING FOR TROUBLE OR SOMETHING.

WELL... ARE YOU?

NOPE! ... BUT, SOMETIMES, IT FINDS ME.

MOM? SOS! THIS IS AN EMERGENCY! CANDACE HALLORAN IS MY ROOMMATE! I DON'T KNOW HOW THIS HAPPENED, BUT IT COULD BE BAD NEWS!

SHE WENT TO SCHOOL WITH ME, REMEMBER? SHE WAS OK IN JUNIOR HIGH BUT THEN SHE SHAVED HER HEAD AN' PIERCED STUFF...

AND SHE'S SO WEIRD, NOW. I DON'T THINK I'LL EVER BE ABLE TO...

HEY, LIZ?

I JUST WANTED TO SAY... IF I HAVE TO LIVE WITH SOMEONE— I'M GLAD IT'S YOU.

DADDY? ELIZABETH READ A BEDTIME STORY TO ME EVERY NIGHT. WILL YOU READ TO ME?

SURE, HONEY.

THEN SHE USED TO TUCK ME IN AND BRING ME A GLASS OF WATER.

AND SHE'D COME TO MY ROOM LATER TO SEE IF I WAS OK.

I CAN DO THAT TOO.

IF I COULDN'T SLEEP, SHE'D LET ME LISTEN TO CD'S AN' RUB MY BACK AN' BRING ME COOKIES!

ELLY...DOES ONE OF MY LEGS LOOK A LOT LONGER THAN THE OTHER?

MOM? UHHH?

I'M SCARED. I DON'T WANNA SLEEP UPSTAIRS BY MY-SELF. I MISS ELIZABETH!

HONEY, ELIZABETH IS IN UNIVERSITY NOW.

I WANT YOU AN' DADDY TO MOVE UPSTAIRS AGAIN. I DON'T **WANNA** BE ALONE!

WHY DON'T YOU GO BACK TO BED, AND I'LL COME AND SLEEP IN ELIZABETH'S ROOM TONIGHT.

SNIFF... OK.

ELLY, WE TALKED ABOUT THIS! APRIL HAS THE DOG IN HER ROOM, SHE HAS HER RADIO, HER TOYS. SHE SAID SHE'D BE FINE!

SHE EVEN SAID SHE WANTED TO BE ALONE-THAT IT WOULD MAKE HER FEEL ALL GROWN UP!

I KNOW.

THESE THINGS ALWAYS WORK WELL IN THEORY.

Lynn

57

I DID IT, MOM! I SLEPT UP-STAIRS ALL BY MYSELF LAST NIGHT.

I'M PROUD OF YOU, APRIL—BUT YOU'VE DONE THAT BEFORE!

IT'S NOT THE SAME NOW.

I KNOW. WE HAVE A WHOLE NEW ROUTINE TO GET USED TO.

NOW THAT LIZ AND MICHAEL ARE GONE, YOU ARE THE NUMBER ONE KID IN THE FAMILY!

AND YOUR FATHER IS NUMBER TWO!

WHATCHA MAKING, DADDY?

AN ENGINEER FOR MY STEAM ENGINE.

I HAVEN'T BEEN ABLE TO FIND ANYTHING "JUST RIGHT," SO I'M MAKING HIM MYSELF.

BUT... HE'S GOT NO LEGS ON HIM!

THAT'S OK—YOU'LL ONLY BE ABLE TO SEE HIM FROM THE WAIST UP!

...IT WAS A "GROUP EFFORT."

I LIKE BEING BACK AT SCHOOL, DON'T YOU, BECKY?

UH-HUH. AN' I LIKE OUR NEW TEACHER, TOO.

I LIKE THE FACT THAT WE'VE GOT ACTUAL COMBINATION LOCKS!

BUT I KEEP FORGETTING THE NUMBERS.

WELL, YOU'VE GOTTA WRITE THEM DOWN SOMEWHERE 'TIL YOU'VE GOT THEM MEMORIZED!

TSK! I DID, DUMMY!

I WROTE THEM ON THE BACK OF THE LOCK!

HOW'S THE ARTICLE COMING, MIKE?

I THOUGHT IT WAS FINISHED, BUT I'M WORKING WITH AN EDITOR WHO KEEPS CHANGING THINGS.

HE CHANGES MY PUNCTUATION, ADDS WORDS I'D NEVER USE AND CROSSES OUT ENTIRE PARAGRAPHS!

WRITING IS AN ART!!! IT'S A FORM OF PERSONAL EXPRESSION! I HATE HAVING MY WORK HACKED UP LIKE THIS!!!

YEAH.

THE GUY WHO SCULPTED THE VENUS DE MILO MUST HAVE WORKED WITH AN EDITOR.

YOUR PHOTOGRAPHS ARE SPECTACULAR, WEED!

WE'VE BOTH PULLED OFF SOME GOOD WORK, MIKE.

TOO BAD WE WON'T SEE IT PUBLISHED UNTIL SPRING.

HEY, ANYTHING WORTHWHILE IS WORTH WAITING FOR.

GREAT...

EVERY TIME I SAY SOMETHING THAT REMINDS HIM OF DEANNA... HIS EYES GLAZE OVER.

BILL, BILL, RECEIPT, BILL, JUNK, JUNK, LETTER FROM HONDURAS...

Dearest Michael,
By the time you receive this, I'll be working in a dispensary in El Progreso.

OUR TRANSLATOR HAS RENTED A ROOM FOR ME NEARBY.

IT WILL BE GOOD TO HAVE AN ACTUAL BED, RUNNING WATER AND A LITTLE PRIVACY FOR A CHANGE.

LIVING AND WORKING IN THE MOUNTAINS WAS AN INCREDIBLE EXPERIENCE. HOW I LOVE THE HONDURAN CHILDREN!

Remember Kevin Smythe? You met him at the airport the day we left.

He and his wife, June, have become great friends and...

HE'S MARRIED! THE GUY I WAS SO WORRIED ABOUT IS MARRIED!!!

MY GUESS IS—IT'S A VICTORY DANCE.

WELL, TELL 'IM 'E'S CRACKIN' ME PLASTER.

In El Progreso, I'll be packaging and dispensing drugs and medical supplies.

IT WILL BE NICE TO HAVE A STERILE ENVIRONMENT AND MODERN EQUIPMENT!

I think about you every day. I can't tell you how much I miss you, Michael.

RATS.

...I WAS HOPING SHE'D TRY!

BEE BOP A LOO SHE'S MUH BAY BEE...

WHAPPITA WHAPPITA WHAP WAPPA WHAP WHAP NAAA

KNOW WHAT, PATTERSON?

YOU'RE EASIER TO LIVE WITH WHEN YOU'RE IN A BAD MOOD.

HI THERE!!

CAN I HELP YOU, MA'AM?

YES— MY FINGERNAILS KEEP BREAKING AND I'M LOOKING FOR SOMETHING TO MAKE THEM STRONGER.

OK. FIRST OF ALL, YOU NEED TO MOISTURIZE AN' DO, LIKE THIS... TOTAL HAND AN' NAIL MASSAGE AT LEAST TWICE A DAY.

ALSO, YOU NEED TO FILE THEM SLOWLY, SIDE TO TOP, WITH A FINE EMERY, LIKE THIS.

THEN, YOU'LL WANT TO USE A NAIL STRENGTHENING COLLAGEN-TYPE UNDERCOAT AN' COVER WITH A NYLON MICRO-FIBER POLISH.

AND DON'T FORGET TO WEAR RUBBER GLOVES 'CAUSE WHAT REALLY WRECKS YOUR NAILS IS HOUSE-WORK AND GARDENING!

SO, DID YOU FIND SOMETHING TO MAKE YOUR NAILS GROW, ELLY?

NO...

I'VE DECIDED THAT SHORT ONES ARE A "BADGE OF HONOR"!

THIS YEAR, CLASS, WE'RE GOING TO LEARN ABOUT OUR LANGUAGE. WE'RE GOING TO STUDY GRAMMAR, SENTENCE STRUCTURE AND VOCABULARY.

IT TAKES THOUSANDS OF YEARS TO DEVELOP A LANGUAGE. OUR ABILITY TO COMMUNICATE WITH OUR VOICES AND IN WRITING MAKES US EXCEPTIONAL ON THIS PLANET!

WE HAVE A **HUGE** VOCABULARY TO CHOOSE FROM! THERE ARE SO MANY DIFFERENT AND EXCITING WAYS YOU CAN EXPRESS YOURSELF!

IF THAT'S TRUE, WHY DO SO MANY KIDS JUST USE 4-LETTER WORDS?

APRIL, YOU HAVE A BEAUTIFUL DESK IN YOUR ROOM. WHY DON'T YOU DO YOUR HOMEWORK THERE?

I HAVE A DESK?!!

SNORT! NO WONDER APRIL DOESN'T WANT TO DO HER HOMEWORK IN HERE!

APRIL, YOUR ROOM IS A **MESS!** YOUR CLOTHES ARE ON THE FLOOR, YOUR TOYS ARE EVERYWHERE!

YOUR BED HASN'T BEEN MADE FOR DAYS, AND I THINK IT'S AN ABSOLUTE **DISGRACE!**

WEIRD

SHE GETS SO EXCITED ABOUT STUFF I ALREADY KNOW.

APRIL, I THOUGHT MOM ASKED YOU TO TIDY UP YOUR ROOM.

I'M GOING TO.

WELL, MAYBE YOU SHOULD START NOW.

DADDY, I SAID I'M **GOING** TO!

APRIL'S CLEANING UP HER ROOM, JOHN. ...WHAT DID YOU SAY TO HER?

"IF YOUR MOM DOESN'T CUT OFF YOUR TV AND ALLOWANCE, THEN I'M **GOING** TO!!"

WHAT ARE YOU THINKING ABOUT, JOHN?

... I WAS WONDERING IF WE'RE TOO LENIENT WITH APRIL.

I THINK WE LET HER GET AWAY WITH A LOT MORE THAN OUR OTHER KIDS DID— WE BOTH HAVE TO TOUGHEN UP AND STOP GIVING IN TO HER.

KNOCK KNOCK

...YOU FIRST

COME ON, APRIL. TIME TO GO BACK TO YOUR ROOM.

UMMH?

UP YOU GET.

CARRY ME, DADDY.

I GUESS THAT WAS ONE MORE "LAST TIME" EVENT, WASN'T IT.

CRUNCH

GNAW GRUNCH CRUNCH

CAYENNE PEPPER

SNIFFFFF

AAHHH SNEEEZE

SNEEEZE SNEEZE SNORK SNF
SNRK SNEEF SNUFF PFTT BBL

SNEEZE!

SNORF! SNEEZE! SNIFF! SNUFF
SPTTT

I SEE THE RABBIT'S BEEN CHEWING THE BASEBOARDS AGAIN.

UNIVERSITY'S NOT LIKE HIGH SCHOOL, SIS — OR EVEN GRADE 13. YOU'VE GOTTA BE MORE FOCUSED. YOU GOTTA BE SERIOUS!

YOU NEED A ROUTINE. YOU HAVE TO REVIEW YOUR NOTES EVERY DAY, STUDY IN THE SAME PLACE EVERY DAY...

AND YOU CAN'T TAKE OFF AND PARTY — EVEN IF THE OTHER KIDS ARE DOING IT! ONLY WHEN YOU FEEL YOU REALLY DESERVE A BREAK — THAT'S WHEN YOU CAN RELAX!

IS THAT WHAT YOU DID?

...THAT'S WHAT I SHOULD HAVE DONE!

HEY, MIKE! — I KNEW YOU GUYS WERE HOME FOR THE WEEKEND!

HOW'S IT GOING, LAWRENCE?

YOUR MOM HAD A SPECTACULAR GARDEN THIS YEAR.

THANKS. — I WAS PLANNING TO COME OVER AS SOON AS I WAS FINISHED HERE,

I LOVE PLANTS, MIKE. GROWING FLOWERS IS LIKE HAVING THE PERFECT RELATIONSHIP. YOU LOVE THEM, NURTURE THEM, THEY GROW AND THEY BLOSSOM...

AND IN THE END, WHEN IT'S OVER... YOU KNOW THEY DIDN'T LEAVE YOU WILLINGLY.

HAVE YOU HEARD FROM DEANNA?

YES, SHE'S IN EL PROGRESO. SHE'S DOING REALLY WELL. I SURE MISS HER.

HAVE YOU HEARD FROM BEN?

HE'S MOVING FROM PARIS TO CHICAGO, MIKE. HE WANTS TO BE A COMPOSER... HE'S MARRIED TO HIS MUSIC.

CHICAGO IS GOOD! AT LEAST YOU'LL BE ON THE SAME CONTINENT!

YES...

...BUT WE LIVE IN TWO SEPARATE WORLDS.

Panel 1: LIFE'S WEIRD, MIKE. ONE DAY YOU'RE HUMMING ALONG AND EVERY— THING'S THE WAY IT ALWAYS WAS...

Panel 2: THEN, SUDDENLY THE ROAD DIVIDES AND YOU FIND YOURSELF TAKING A TOTALLY DIFFERENT PATH.

Panel 3: AND IT'S AS IF EVERY— THING IN THE PAST WAS PREPARING YOU FOR WHAT'S AHEAD... BUT YOU STILL CAN'T QUITE SEE PAST THE BENDS IN THE ROAD!

Panel 4: DO YOU KNOW WHAT I MEAN?

NOPE. I'M LOST.

Panel 5: ME TOO... BUT AT LEAST I KNOW I'M GOING IN THE RIGHT DIRECTION!

Panel 6: I'VE MADE SOME MAJOR DECISIONS, MIKE. THE FIRST ONE IS TO BREAK OFF WITH BEN.

Panel 7: I'LL ALWAYS CARE FOR HIM, BUT WE LEAD SUCH DIFFERENT LIVES AND I'VE LEARNED THAT YOU HAVE TO LET GO.

Panel 8: I'VE DECIDED TO SPE— CIALIZE IN BONSAI AND MINIATURE PLANTS ... AND I'VE DECIDED TO GET TO KNOW MY FATHER.

Panel 9: YOU MET YOUR FATHER? LAWRENCE, THAT'S AMAZING!— WHAT'S HE LIKE?!!

I'M NOT SURE YET...

Panel 10: ...HE'S STILL GETTING OVER THE SHOCK OF MEETING ME!

Panel 11: REMEMBER DURING THE SUMMER I TOLD YOU ABOUT MY FATHER AND HOW HE AND MY MOTHER MET?

YES. YOU SAID HE'S A SPECIAL— IST IN TROPICAL DISEASES.

Panel 12: ISN'T HE COMING TO TORON— TO TO GIVE A LECTURE?

YES. I MET HIM AT THE AIRPORT.

Panel 13: WHAT?!! YOU WALKED UP TO A COMPLETE STRANGER AND SAID, "HELLO, DR. DASILVA—I'M YOUR SON?!!!"

NO...

Panel 14: I WALKED UP TO A COM— PLETE STRANGER AND SAID, "HELLO, DR. DA SILVA ... I'M YOUR CHAUFFEUR."

WHEN I FOUND OUT MY FATHER WAS COMING TO TORONTO, I KNEW I HAD TO MEET HIM, BUT I DIDN'T KNOW HOW!

SO, I CALLED A FRIEND IN THE BIOLOGY DEPARTMENT AT THE UNIVERSITY AND SHE GOT ME ALL HIS FLIGHT INFORMATION.

THEN I RENTED A BLACK SUIT AND A LIMO AND WENT TO THE INTERNATIONAL ARRIVALS GATE.

YOU MEAN YOU KIDNAPPED HIM?!!

NOT EXACTLY, MIKE... I MEAN, I WAS THE KID!

THE UNIVERSITY HAD ALREADY HIRED A LIMO SERVICE, BUT I TOLD THE DRIVER I WAS PLAYING A PRACTICAL JOKE ON MY DAD. I GAVE HIM 100 BUCKS TO LET ME TAKE HIS PLACE.

WAITING FOR THOSE DOORS TO OPEN TOOK AN ETERNITY. MY HEART POUNDED SO HARD, I THOUGHT EVERYONE AROUND ME COULD HEAR...

THEN I SAW HIM.

DR. DASILVA? I'M LAWRENCE POIRIER.

POIRIER! THAT WILL BE EASY TO REMEMBER.

DR. DASILVA

...I ONCE KNEW SOMEONE BY THAT NAME.

BAGGAGE

IT'S ABOUT A 30-MINUTE RIDE FROM THE AIRPORT TO DOWNTOWN. WE TALKED ABOUT THE USUAL THINGS.

WET DAY! AND WINDY.

I KEPT SEEING HIS FACE IN THE REAR VIEW MIRROR AND I WANTED TO SCREAM -"DR. DASILVA! LOOK AT ME! WE HAVE THE SAME EYES, THE SAME MOUTH!!!"

BUT HE SAID IT FIRST:

LAWRENCE, WE'VE NEVER MET BEFORE...

BUT YOU LOOK REMARKABLY LIKE ONE OF MY SONS!

I DROVE HIM TO THE HOTEL AND WAITED WHILE HE CHECKED IN.

AND HE STILL DIDN'T KNOW WHO YOU WERE?

I OFFERED TO CARRY HIS SUITCASE UP TO HIS ROOM, AND THE TWO OF US GOT INTO THE ELEVATOR.

WHEN WE STEPPED OUT AT THE 6TH FLOOR, THERE WAS A LARGE MIRROR ON THE WALL IN FRONT OF US...

MY GOD!

I HAD A SPEECH PLANNED, BUT WHAT DO YOU SAY TO A MAN WHO IS LOOKING AT HIS 23-YEAR-OLD SON FOR THE FIRST TIME?

I THOUGHT HE'D BE ANGRY. HE COULD HAVE HAD ME ARRESTED FOR IMPERSONATING HIS DRIVER.

HE UNLOCKED THE DOOR TO HIS HOTEL ROOM AND PUT HIS THINGS ON THE BED...

AND HE SAID NOTHING TO YOU?

TWO WORDS.

... I'M SORRY.

THE DEAN WAS EXPECTING TO MEET HIM AT THE UNIVERSITY.

THIS IS DR. DASILVA. I WILL BE A BIT LATE.

HE ASKED ME TO SIT DOWN. HE TOOK A PHOTO OUT OF HIS WALLET AND HANDED IT TO ME.

I HAVE TWO BROTHERS, ANDRÉ AND RICARDO.

DID YOU ASK HIM WHY HE ABANDONED YOUR MOM? DID YOU ASK WHY HE NEVER ACKNOWLEDGED YOU?!!!

MY MOTHER NAMED ME AFTER THE ST. LAWRENCE RIVER, MICHAEL...

AND AFTER I HAD MET HIM, ALL OF THAT WAS JUST WATER UNDER THE BRIDGE.

HE TOLD ME THAT HE'D LOVED MY MOTHER. HE SAID HE CALLED HER "CONEJA".

WHEN SHE LEFT ECUADOR, I WANTED TO GO WITH HER, ...BUT I WOULD NEVER HAVE SURVIVED IN HER WORLD, JUST AS SHE WOULD NEVER HAVE FIT INTO MINE.

I UNDERSTOOD WHAT HE WAS SAYING. SOME RELATIONSHIPS ARE JUST PLAIN FANTASY.

THE TROUBLE FOR BOTH OF US IS... I'M A FACT!

HE LOOKED AT MY SUIT AND HE SMILED. HE SAID THAT PRETENDING TO BE HIS CHAUFFEUR WAS A BRILLIANT IDEA AND HE WAS PROUD OF ME FOR THINKING OF IT.

WE TALKED FOR AN HOUR AND THEN I DROVE HIM TO THE UNIVERSITY.

WELL, NOW - WHAT SHALL I DO... GIVE YOU A TIP?

NO, SIR. THAT ISN'T NECESSARY.

A HANDSHAKE WILL DO.

SO, YOU'VE MET YOUR FATHER!

YES-AND I'LL SEE HIM AGAIN BEFORE HE GOES BACK TO BRAZIL.

AND YOUR MOTHER?

SHE'S COMING WITH ME.

LAWRENCE, I'M SURPRISED BY HOW VERY CIVILIZED YOU'VE ALL BEEN!—FOR SOME PEOPLE, THIS WOULD HAVE TURNED OUT LIKE A BAD MOVIE!

THAT'S THE BEST THING I DISCOVERED ABOUT MY FAMILY, MIKE...

...WE'RE A CLASS ACT.

75

MAGAZINES
SMOKES
CANDY
LOTTO *LOU'S*
POP
SNACKS

VISA

Callahan's

LOU'S LOT

Hmmm

BE A LOVE SAVAGE. CAPTURE HIM WITH THE **SIN**SATIONAL SCENT OF "AGGRESSION"

WHAT MEN WANT AND HOW TO GIVE IT TO THEM! DRIVE HIM MAD WITH *"Entice"* APHRODISIACS YOU CAN MAKE AT HOME.

FASHION STATEMENT

50 SENSUOUS WAYS TO GET HIS ATTENTION. LASHES THAT LURE. HOW TO SNAG AND KEEP "MR. RIGHT"

WOMEN'S WORLD

HOT, HOT, HOT ROMANCE SECRETS. "NEW MOVES." BE IRRESISTIBLE IN BRAZEN LINGERIE!

frosty

EVER READ THE STUFF IN THESE WOMEN'S MAGAZINES, LOU?

YEAH, AMAZING, ISN'T IT?

frosty

AFTER ALL THEM TRICKS PAY OFF AN' THEY'VE BEEN MARRIED AWHILE...

THEY WANNA PROVE THEIR LOVE TO YOU BY **COOKING**!

Lynn

GRAMPA'S COMING FOR CHRISTMAS! GRAMPA'S COMING FOR CHRISTMAS!

WHEN WILL HE GET HERE? IS HE BRINGING HIS DOG? HOW LONG CAN HE STAY?

I DON'T KNOW, HONEY.

AS SOON AS HE'S MADE HIS TRAVEL ARRANGEMENTS, HE'S GOING TO CALL.

GRAMPA'S COMING FOR CHRISTMAS! GRAMPA'S COMING! ♪

APRIL, SETTLE DOWN! YOU'RE JUMPING AND TWIRLING ALL OVER THE HOUSE—AND YOU'RE MAKING ME CRAZY!

I'M SORRY—I CAN'T HELP IT!

I'VE GOT TOO MUCH HAPPY INSIDE!!

PEPPERONI STICK, CHEESE 'N' CRACKERS, JUICE BOX, GRANOLA BAR!

LOOK, MOM—I MADE MY OWN LUNCH!

GOOD FOR YOU! CAN I SEE?

HOW ABOUT ADDING AN APPLE OR AN ORANGE...AND SOME CARROT STICKS?

I LIKE TO KNOW YOU HAVE SOME HEALTHY NATURAL FOODS IN THERE!

...I ALSO LIKE TO BELIEVE THAT YOU EAT THEM.

THE COMBINATION TO MY LOCK IS EASY TO REMEMBER. IT'S 2-11-22.

MINE'S EASIER!

MY NUMBERS ARE 12-20-12!

MINE'S 6-31-8. —MY SISTER'S AGE, MY MOM'S AGE AN MY AGE!

MY COMBINATION IS 36-24-34

EWWW!

HOW ARE YOU SUPPOSED TO REMEMBER THAT?!!

Cc Dd Ee Ff Gg

39 564
27 +27

52
61

Dd Ee Ff Gg

OK, APRIL AND GERALD... YOU CAN EACH DO FOUR EXTRA MATH PROBLEMS AT HOME TONIGHT.

HOW DO THEY KNOW?

I DUNNO... THEY JUST DO.

HOW WAS SCHOOL TODAY, APRIL?

OK— EXCEPT FOR ENGLISH. WE HAD TO DRAW CIRCLES AN' LOOPS, CIRCLES AN' LOOPS...

FOR HOMEWORK, WE HAFTA MAKE ROWS AN' ROWS OF ALPHABET LETTERS.

THEN WHEN WE KNOW HOW TO DO THEM RIGHT, WE'RE SUPPOSED TO JOIN THEM TOGETHER.

THAT'S CALLED "CURSIVE" WRITING!

REALLY?!

*✻✱⊘

THEN, WITH OUR BOYS IN CONTROL OF THIS STRATEGIC AREA, WE PUSHED FORWARD...

RATTA-TATTAT TATTA POP POP?P BWANG! RATTATA TTATAT ATATTATT

DADDY, ON JUST ABOUT EVERY TV STATION, THERE'S STUFF ABOUT THE WAR.

I KNOW.

YOUR GRANDPA FOUGHT IN THE LAST WORLD WAR, APRIL.

DID HE SHOOT ANYBODY?

YES, HE DID.

REALLY?!

HE HAD TO, OR THE OTHER SOLDIER WOULD HAVE SHOT HIM.

WOW! GRANDPA NEVER TOLD ME ABOUT THAT!

I KNOW. HE DOESN'T LIKE TO TALK ABOUT IT... HE SAYS IT'S JUST TOO PAINFUL.

THEN, WHY DO THEY SHOW THE WAR ON TV?

BECAUSE IT WAS FOUGHT FOR OUR FREEDOM AND ALLOWS US TO LIVE THE WAY WE DO TODAY.

STRANGE, ISN'T IT... THAT SOMETHING SO IMPORTANT FOR **US** TO REMEMBER...

IS SOMETHING THAT OTHERS TRY SO HARD TO FORGET.

Lynn

81

HI, ELIZABETH! GUESS WHAT? GRAMPA JIM IS COMING FOR CHRISTMAS AND HE'S BRINGING HIS DOG, DIXIE — ISN'T THAT COOL?

SCHOOL IS OK EXCEPT THERE'S A BOY CALLED GERALD WHO BUGS ME. WE HAVE STARTED TO LEARN HOW TO ACTUALLY WRITE WORDS BY CONNECTING THE LETTERS TOGETHER.

THAT'S WHY I'M SENDING YOU THIS INSTEAD OF E-MAIL BECAUSE MY TEACHER SAYS I HAVE TO PRACTICE!!!!!

SO — HOW DO YOU LIKE MY SIGNATURE?!

♡ april

Lynn

I WISH CANDACE DIDN'T TAKE SO LONG IN THE BATHROOM. IT'LL BE FULL OF STEAM WHEN I GET IN THERE

SHE ALSO LEAVES HER TOWEL ON THE FLOOR AN' NEVER PUTS THE LID BACK ON THE SHAMPOO.

I WISH SHE'D DO THE DISHES MORE. AN' I'M NOT CRAZY ABOUT HER MUSIC.

IT'S NOT EASY GETTING USED TO SOMEONE ELSE'S HABITS AND SOMEONE ELSE'S STUFF.

MAN, IF IT'S THIS HARD TO ADJUST TO A ROOMMATE... WHAT'S IT LIKE TO GET MARRIED!!

HEY, LIZ — YOU WANNA HEAD DOWNTOWN WITH ME? WE'RE OUTTA GROCERIES AN' I NEED SOME CASH.

UH, SURE!

PLE... RETURN ALL MANUALS TO THE LIBRA...

HOW LONG ARE YOU GONNA BE?

ABOUT 2 SECONDS... I'M ALMOST DONE.

FOR STU... USE ON...

OK, BUT I WANNA GET THE 5 O'CLOCK BUS. IF YOU'RE NOT BACK AT THE REZ BY...

I'M TYPING AS FAST AS I CAN!

FOR STUD USE ONL...

THAT WAS MY AUNT RUBY ON THE PHONE, LIZ. SHE OWNS A CORNER STORE DOWN NEAR THE OVER-PASS.

SHE LIVES IN THE BACK. SHE SAID IF WE WANTED TO HIT HER PLACE FOR DINNER, IT WOULD BE COOL.

SOUNDS GOOD!

ARE YOU GONNA GO OUT DRESSED LIKE THAT?

SURE, WHY NOT?

PEOPLE MIGHT THINK YOU'RE ECCENTRIC.

IT MUST BE NICE HAVING YOUR AUNT RUBY IN TOWN.

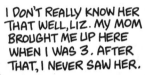

I DON'T REALLY KNOW HER THAT WELL, LIZ. MY MOM BROUGHT ME UP HERE WHEN I WAS 3. AFTER THAT, I NEVER SAW HER.

BUT, FOR YEARS, I REMEM-BERED HER STORE!

HOW COME?

THE PENNY CANDY COUNTER WAS HUGE... AND AT EYE LEVEL!

RUBY, THIS IS MY FRIEND, ELIZABETH.

HEY, IT'S A PLEASURE...

I PUT A CASSEROLE ON, BUT WE CAN'T EAT 'TIL MY PART-TIMER COMES IN. DO YOU MIND?

NAH!

YOU COULD SELL ME A PACK OF BUTTS WHILE WE'RE WAITING.

WHY DO YOU SMOKE THOSE THINGS—YOU WANT TO DIE?

WHY DO YOU SELL THEM?

... IT'S A LIVING.

THIS IS YOUR CHICKEN SURPRISE. THE SURPRISE WILL BE IF IT'S EDIBLE.

SO, HERE I HAVE MY SISTER'S KID-SITTING AT MY TABLE ...ALL GROWN UP AN' IN UNIVERSITY.

TELL ME WHERE YOU'RE HEADED, CANDACE-WHAT'S YOUR PLAN?

I THOUGHT I'D GO INTO PSYCHOLOGY... DO YOU THINK THAT'S A GOOD IDEA?

...DEPENDS ON WHAT YOU'RE LIKE WHEN YOU GET OUT!

CANDACE IS GOING TO BE A PSYCHOLOGIST AND ELIZABETH IS GOING TO BE A TEACHER. WELL...I'M PROUD OF YOU BOTH.

I NEVER FINISHED SCHOOL, SO HERE I AM RUNNING A CORNER STORE. — BUT, I'VE BEEN HERE OVER 20 YEARS. I KNOW THE NEIGHBORHOOD...

I KNOW WHO'S SICK AN' WHO'S BETTER. I KNOW WHO'S GETTING MARRIED OR HAVING A BABY.

FOLKS COME IN IF THEY NEED A FRIEND OR A LITTLE CREDIT OR JUST TO HANG AROUND.

IN OTHER WORDS, YOU'RE A BUSINESS-WOMAN, A TEACHER AND A PSYCHOLOGIST!

WELL, THAT WAS SUPPER. YOU CAN CHECK OUT FRONT FOR DESSERT.

REALLY? WHAT CAN WE HAVE?

I DON'T CARE. ICE CREAM, CANDY, CHIPS- WHATEVER YOU WANT.

WE SHOULD PAY FOR THIS STUFF...LIKE, YOU CAN'T JUST GIVE IT TO US FOR FREE!

DON'T WORRY. IT'S TAKEN CARE OF.

I WORK ON THE BARTER SYSTEM.

WELL, I CAN'T SIT STILL ANY LONGER, CANDACE, I'M YOUR AUNT—I'M NOT YOUR MOM, SO I HAVE NO BUSINESS SAYING THIS...

BUT YOU LOOK LIKE YOU WERE ATTACKED BY A LAWNMOWER... LIKE A KIWI FRUIT WITH BANGS —KNOW WHAT I MEAN?

YOU HAD THE MOST BEAUTIFUL CURLY HAIR. WHY ON EARTH WOULD YOU SHAVE IT ALL OFF?!!

EVER NOTICE HOW PEOPLE WHO ADMIT THEY HAVE NO BUSINESS SAYING SOMETHING GO AHEAD AND SAY IT ANYWAY?...

AND WHILE I'M ON THE SUBJECT—I'VE GOTTA ASK ABOUT THE BLACK MASCARA, THE VAMPIRE LIPS, THE NOSE RING AND TATTOO.

YOU'RE A BEAUTIFUL GIRL! WHAT ON EARTH ARE YOU DOING?

IT'S DECORATION, AUNT RUBY. AND IT'S MY BODY!!!

WHAT'S WRONG WITH DECORATING IT UP A LITTLE?!!

BECAUSE, HONEY...IT'S LIKE SPRAYPAINTING A ROSE.

COME BACK ANY TIME, YOU HEAR? CALL ME IF YOU NEED ANYTHING.

BYE!

THANKS FOR DINNER.

I LIKE YOUR AUNT RUBY, CANDACE.

SHE'S OK FOR A RELATIVE.

I THINK I'M GONNA STAY AT HER PLACE OVER CHRISTMAS.

YOU'RE NOT GOING HOME?

AS FAR AS I'M CONCERNED, LIZ...HOME IS WHERE I HANG MY HAT.

YEAH, ME TOO.

BUT I THINK I'LL ALWAYS KEEP AN EXTRA ONE AT MY PARENTS' PLACE.

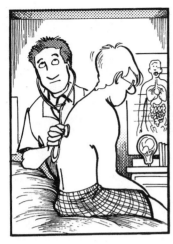

WELL, JOHN—I'D SAY YOU'RE IN PRETTY GOOD SHAPE FOR A MAN YOUR AGE.

SORRY. I'LL HAVE TO STOP SAYING THINGS LIKE THAT!

YOU WILL...

... WHEN YOU'RE A MAN MY AGE.

SO, I'M IN GOOD HEALTH, BUT MY CHOLESTEROL IS HIGH.

YOU GOT IT! HERE'S A LIST OF FOODS YOU SHOULD AVOID.

BUT THESE ARE ALL THE THINGS THAT I LOVE!!!

WELL, IF YOU CAN'T AVOID THEM, YOU SHOULD AT LEAST CUT DOWN.

I'LL HAVE A PLAIN SALAD AND ONE FRY.

ONE FRY? WE'RE TALKING ONE FRENCH FRY ONLY?

YES.

CREATE YOUR OWN SANDWICH

WE AIM TO CHEESE

YOU WANT GRAVY WITH THAT?

I DON'T PARTY ANYMORE, TED. I DON'T DRINK OR SMOKE OR GAMBLE.

YOU'D THINK I COULD AT LEAST ENJOY THE FOODS I LIKE BEST!

HIGH CHOLESTEROL, HUH?

AND ELLY IS A GREAT COOK! SHE MAKES ROASTS, SAUCES, BUNS, CHEESECAKE. MY WIFE IS AN EXCELLENT COOK!

REALLY?

BUMMER.

DADDY, DADDY—GUESS WHAT! WE'RE HAVING MACARONI AN' CHEESE FOR SUPPER... YOUR FAVORITE!

ELLY, I SAW THE DOCTOR TODAY. HE SAYS MY CHOLESTEROL IS TOO HIGH.

OH!

WELL, AFTER A STATEMENT LIKE THAT, I GUESS I CAN'T SERVE YOU MUCH OF THIS!

THAT WASN'T A STATEMENT... THAT WAS A SENTENCE!

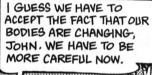
I GUESS WE HAVE TO ACCEPT THE FACT THAT OUR BODIES ARE CHANGING, JOHN. WE HAVE TO BE MORE CAREFUL NOW.

I HATE THE WORDS "MIDDLE-AGED." I DON'T **FEEL** MIDDLE-AGED. I'M EXACTLY THE SAME PERSON I WAS WHEN I WAS 30!

NO YOU'RE NOT! YOU'RE MORE MATURE, MORE CONFIDENT, MORE EXPERIENCED—YOU'RE BETTER
... WE'RE BOTH BETTER!

WE ARE THE ONLY PRODUCTS THAT TEND TO IMPROVE WHILE THE PACKAGING DETERIORATES.

YOU STILL THINK I LOOK OK?
YOU LOOK GREAT.

WHAT ABOUT THE GREY HAIR?
IT'S SILVER... AND EXTREMELY ATTRACTIVE.

HOW ABOUT THE SAGGING CHIN?
JOHN, YOU HAVE AN EXPRESSIVE FACE WITH LOTS OF CHARACTER.

I'M GLAD YOU CAN LOVE ALL MY SAGS, BAGS, ROLLS AND WRINKLES, ELLY.
MMM

...BUT I HATE THEM ON ME!

Panel 1: NOBODY LIKES THEIR OWN LOOKS, EL. I'VE GOT A SQUARE FACE, NO CHIN AND A BODY THAT'S SHAPED LIKE A FIRE PLUG.

Panel 2: WELL, I HATE MY NOSE, MY CHEST IS FLAT, MY HAIR IS MOUSY AND ONE OF MY EYES IS HIGHER THAN THE OTHER...

Café Ole

Panel 3: WHEN YOU THINK ABOUT IT, EL— THERE IS SOMETHING GOOD ABOUT BEING OLD...

Panel 4: EVENTUALLY, WE ALL START TO LOOK THE SAME.

Panel 5: I'M GLAD YOU'VE DECIDED TO WORK OUT WITH ME AGAIN, EL. HERE'S AN OUTFIT YOU CAN WEAR.

Panel 6: HOW DO YOU FIT INTO THIS? IT'S SPANDEX. IT STRETCHES TO FIT ANY SHAPE. TRY IT ON!

Panel 7: CONNIE, THIS MAKES ME LOOK LIKE A FAT, STRING-WRAPPED DELI-CHEESE. RIGHT...

Panel 8: I CALL THAT SUCKER THE MOTIVATOR.

Panel 9: HI THERE! WHERE WERE YOU? OVER AT CONNIE'S HOUSE, EXERCISING!

Panel 10: IF I CAN'T STOP THE AGING PROCESS, I SHOULD AT LEAST TRY AND SLOW IT DOWN A LITTLE.

Panel 11: BECAUSE, BELIEVE IT OR NOT, YOU'RE STILL MARRIED TO A VIBRANT, ACTIVE AND SEXY WOMAN.

Panel 12: SNORGKK

THE VIAGRA GENERATION

Summer Clothes

Summer toys

Summer

SNAP!

SNAP!

SNAP!

ERK? BLEAH

GALOOP GALORUP GULPP GALOOP

I'M SO GLAD YOU COULD COME FOR CHRISTMAS, DAD. WE'VE GOT YOUR ROOM ALL READY.

AIRPORT PARKING

I'VE BEEN LOOKING FORWARD TO THIS TRIP, ELLY. I CAN'T WAIT TO SEE APRIL. I BET SHE'S GROWN!

I'M LOOKING FORWARD TO THOSE WIDE EYES AND "HI-YA, GRAMPA!" AND GETTING A GREAT BIG HUG!

DIXIE!!!

GRAMPA, I'M SO HAPPY TO SEE YOU!

MY, YOU'RE GETTING TALL!

HOW COME YOU'VE GOT SO MANY SUITCASES?

APRIL! — YOU DON'T ASK QUESTIONS LIKE THAT AT CHRISTMAS!

HOW COME THEY'RE SO HEAVY? WHAT'S IN THE BIG ONE?!

HONEY, GO ASK YOUR MOM TO PUT ON SOME TEA.

CAN'T I HELP YOU UNPACK?

DIXIE, YOU REMEMBER EDGAR, DON'T YOU, GIRL!

EDDY, YOU REMEMBER DIXIE!

RRRR

ELLY, MAYBE YOU SHOULD FEED THEM AND THEN LET THEM SNIFF AROUND AND GET TO KNOW EACH OTHER!!

SLUPP·MUNCH GULP·SMACK! EAT·CRUNCH! SNARF GLUP EAT!! CHEW GLUT GULP

Dixie

EDGAR

I LEARNED THAT AT A FEW BUSINESS MEETINGS.

SNOOF?

IT'S SO GOOD TO BE HERE, ELLY. LIFE IS AWFULLY QUIET FOR ME THESE DAYS.

WELL, YOU'RE GOING TO BE IN THE MIDDLE OF A CYCLONE SOON, DAD. ELIZABETH COMES HOME FROM UNIVERSITY NEXT WEEK.

AN' MICHAEL'S GIRLFRIEND COMES HOME FROM HONDURAS TOMORROW!

WELL, HE MUST BE EXCITED!

MIKE... CLOCKS GO FASTER WHEN YOU DON'T LOOK AT THEM.

LYNN

I'M GLAD YOU COULD COME TO THE AIRPORT WITH US, MICHAEL. DEANNA WILL BE SO HAPPY TO SEE YOU.

INTERNATIONAL ARRIV

I'LL ADMIT, WE'VE BEEN WORRIED—BUT SHE INSISTED ON GOING! SHE WANTED AN ADVENTURE AND WE HAD TO LET HER GO.

DEANNA!

MICHAEL!

SPEAKING OF LETTING GO...

▷ GROUND TRANSPORTATION ▷

LYNN

MOM, DAD— I HAVE SO MUCH TO TELL YOU! I HAVE SO MANY SOUVENIRS, SO MANY PHOTOGRAPHS...

YOU WON'T BELIEVE WHAT I SAW AND WHAT I LEARNED IN HONDURAS! I'VE COME HOME A DIFFERENT PERSON.

I'VE COME HOME WITH A NEW RESPECT FOR LIFE. I'VE COME HOME WITH A NEW PERSPECTIVE ON EVERYTHING!

OH, DEANNA...

...YOU'VE COME HOME!

ELEVATORS TO PAR

LYNN

ISN'T THIS A BEAUTIFULLY DECORATED WINDOW, GUYS?

IT'S AMAZING, GORD!

MICHAEL, WHAT ARE YOU DOING?

I'M LOOKING AT IT FROM THE RIGHT HEIGHT!

THIS IS HOW I REMEMBER LOOKING AT CHRISTMAS WINDOWS WHEN I WAS SMALL. EVERYTHING SEEMED SO REAL TO ME!

HOW I'D LOVE TO BE ABLE TO SEE FROM THE PERSPECTIVE OF A CHILD AGAIN!

DADDY?...

LIFT ME UP!

YOU SURE YOU'RE GONNA BE OK, CANDACE?

— HEY, I'LL BE WITH AUNT RUBY. IT'LL BE COOL.

IT'S GONNA BE JUST THE TWO OF US.

MY HOUSE IS GONNA BE PACKED!

GRANDPA JIM IS THERE WITH HIS DOG, MY BROTHER'S COMING HOME WITH HIS GIRLFRIEND, MY UNCLE PHIL AND AUNT GEORGIA WILL BE THERE,

SOUNDS LIKE CHAOS!

...SOUNDS LIKE CHRISTMAS!

DEANNA, WHAT IN THE WORLD IS THIS?

SOAP! I THINK IT'S MADE FROM FAT, LYE AND ASHES.

I BOUGHT A HAND-EMBROIDERED SHAWL ... AND THESE ARE PIECES OF OPAL!

I BROUGHT SO MANY THINGS BACK FROM HONDURAS...

WHERE ARE YOUR CLOTHES AND YOUR SHOES?

I ALSO LEFT A LOT BEHIND.

LOOK AT ALL THE STUFF IN MY CLOSET! I OWN TOO MANY THINGS!

DO YOU KNOW THERE ARE KIDS WHO HAVE NEVER OWNED A PAIR OF SHOES? SOME PEOPLE HAVE NO CLOTHES EXCEPT FOR WHAT THEY'RE WEARING!

WE ARE ACCUSTOMED TO SUCH EXTRAVAGANCE!

HONEY, RELAX, THEY TOLD YOU THIS WOULD HAPPEN.

IT'S JUST EASY TO BE ANGRY WITH THE WORLD WHEN YOU COME HOME AFTER LIVING IN A POOR COUNTRY.

HOW HAVE I MISSED THEE? LET ME COUNT THE WAYS...

I LOVE THE WAY YOU SAY THINGS, MICHAEL

WHEN I WAS IN HONDURAS, I'D LOOK UP AT THE STARS AT NIGHT AND TRY TO REMEMBER EVERYTHING ABOUT YOU—YOUR FACE, YOUR VOICE, THE SMELL OF YOUR HAIR...

AND I SAID TO MYSELF— "YES". I WANT THIS MAN. HE FEELS RIGHT. I'M SAFE IN THIS RELATIONSHIP.

DEANNA...I LOVE THE WAY YOU SAY THINGS.

SHRIEK!!! GIGGLE GIGGLE GIGGLE

APRIL, STOP RUNNING AROUND THE HOUSE WITH THE DOGS! THEY'RE GETTING OUT OF CONTROL!

FOR HEAVEN'S SAKE, OPEN THE DOOR AND LET THEM OUT BEFORE THEY KNOCK SOMETHING OVER!

AAAUGH!

MOM! MOM! ELIZABETH'S HERE! SHE GOT A RIDE HOME FROM THE BUS!

HONEY, YOU'RE EARLY! WE DIDN'T EXPECT YOU UNTIL TOMORROW!

I KNOW—I JUST COULDN'T WAIT ANOTHER DAY.

IT'S LIKE I'M SOME KIND OF VEHICLE THAT GOES GREAT FOR A WHILE—BUT RUNS OUT OF GAS...

AND THE ONLY THING TO DO IS COME HOME AND "FILL UP" ON FAMILY!

ZZZZTTTT!

YOU DO A BEAUTIFUL JOB OF WRAPPING GIFTS, MOM.

THANK YOU, ELIZABETH!

MOST PEOPLE JUST BUY THOSE PRETTY BAGS AND PUT THE GIFT INSIDE WITH SOME TISSUE.

YOU GO TO SO MUCH TROUBLE... AND IT ALL GETS TORN APART LATER!

I KNOW, BUT I LIKE TO PUT A LITTLE EXTRA EFFORT INTO GIFT-GIVING.

I CHOOSE SPECIAL PAPERS, I BUY NICE RIBBON, I MAKE ALL MY OWN BOWS.

I WANT EACH GIFT TO BE A PERSONAL, LOVING EXPRESSION OF AFFECTION.

COOL.

SO HOW MUCH IS THERE LEFT TO WRAP?

INLINE SKATES

SUPER ROAD RACE

HOBBY TOOLS

JEWELL SHOP

POP CORN

AND GIVE ME 6 MORE OF THE MID-SIZED...

WELL, THAT'S GOT THE KITCHEN CLEANED UP... ANYTHING ELSE NEED DOING, SIS?

YEAH.

I'VE GOTTA ASK, MIKE... WHAT'S HAPPENING WITH YOU AND DEANNA? IS SHE GONNA BE MY SISTER-IN-LAW? ...BECAUSE I REALLY WANT THAT TO HAPPEN!

WELL, WE'RE KIND OF THINKING WE MIGHT GET MARRIED SOME-TIME. BUT WE'RE NOT READY TO SAY ANYTHING YET. SO — KEEP IT UNDER YOUR HAT!

... I DON'T WEAR HATS.

DADDY, I CAN'T WAIT 'TIL TOMORROW—CAN I OPEN A PRESENT TONIGHT? PLEASE, PLEASE, PLEASE?

WELL, I SUPPOSE...

YAH!

CASTLE BUILDING BLOX

WHAT ARE YOU DOING NOW, APRIL?

WRAPPING IT UP AGAIN.

THIS ISN'T THE ONE I MEANT TO OPEN.

FOR WHAT WE ARE ABOUT TO RECEIVE... AND FOR WHAT SOME OF US HAVE ALREADY RECEIVED... MAY THE LORD MAKE US TRULY THANKFUL.

DADDY, WHEN WE WENT TO PHILPOTTS DEPARTMENT STORE, SANTA WAS THERE—AND WHEN WE WENT TO EASTGATE MALL—HE WAS THERE, TOO!

LOK-BLOKS

...HOW CAN HE BE IN TWO PLACES AT ONCE?

DOES SANTA REALLY LIVE AT THE NORTH POLE, DADDY? DOES HE REALLY HAVE REINDEER? CAN THEY ACTUALLY FLY?

HOW CAN HIS SLEIGH CARRY SO MUCH? HOW CAN HE GO TO EVERY HOUSE IN THE WORLD IN ONE NIGHT?

DOES HE MAKE ALL THOSE TOYS IN A FACTORY? DOES HE HAVE ELVES?

HOW DOES HE GO DOWN CHIMNEYS? HOW DOES HE GET INTO HOUSES THAT DON'T HAVE CHIMNEYS?

WELL, I DON'T KNOW, APRIL...

I DO—IT'S **MAGIC!**

MAGIC IS **REAL**, ISN'T IT, DADDY?!

OF COURSE IT IS, HONEY!

EVERY NOW AND THEN, I JUST NEED TO BE REMINDED.

LYNN

HELLO THERE.

HI, I'M ANTHONY. I CAME TO SEE ELIZABETH.

ANTHONY! I REMEMBER YOU—ARE YOU AND ELIZABETH STILL SEEING EACH OTHER?

WELL, WE'RE NOT EXACTLY SEEING EACH OTHER, MR. RICHARDS.

YOU CAME TO SEE ELIZABETH, BUT YOU'RE NOT SEEING EACH OTHER.

NOT EXACTLY, GRANDPA.

I SEE.

HOW WAS YOUR CHRISTMAS, LIZ?

GREAT. I REALLY NEEDED A "FAMILY FIX."

ME TOO... I NEVER THOUGHT YOU COULD BE LONELY AT UNIVERSITY.

YEAH. IT'S WEIRD.

SO YOU HAVEN'T "DATED" ANYBODY?

NO. HAVE YOU?

NO.

IF THOSE TWO AREN'T "SEEING" EACH OTHER... IT'S BECAUSE THEY'VE GOT THEIR EYES SHUT!

YOUR KIDS ARE SURE GROWING UP, ELLY. THERE GOES ELIZABETH WITH HER YOUNG MAN.

AND SHE TELLS ME MICHAEL AND DEANNA ARE ENGAGED!

WHAT?!

THEY'RE "PROMISED," AREN'T THEY?

THEY HAVE AN "UNDERSTANDING"

THEY'VE TALKED ABOUT IT, DAD—BUT IT'S NOT OFFICIAL. THEY'VE MADE NO ANNOUNCEMENT... HE HASN'T GIVEN HER A RING!

DO YOU THINK SHE'LL LIKE IT, TRACEY?

MICHAEL... IT'S BEAUTIFUL!

WHEN ARE YOU GOING TO GIVE IT TO HER?

NEW YEAR'S EVE.

THAT'S TOMORROW, TRACE!

YOU MEAN... AT OUR PLACE?!

MICHAEL, WE ARE HONORED! THIS IS SO EXCITING!

I'M JUST SCARED TO DEATH! WHAT IF SHE SAYS "NO"?

YEAH, THAT'S ALWAYS A POSSIBILITY, MAN.

BUT, HEY-IF YOU'RE GONNA BE HUMILIATED, AT LEAST YOU'LL BE SURROUNDED BY FRIENDS!

HAPPY NEW YEAR!

IT'S 2000! IT'S 2000 EVERYBODY!

12-31

IT'S AN AMAZING NIGHT, MICHAEL, HERE WE ARE TOGETHER, CELEBRATING THE ACTUAL TURN OF THE CENTURY!

IT'S SOMETHING WE'LL BE ABLE TO TELL OUR CHILDREN AND OUR GRANDCHILDREN AND OUR GREAT-GRAND-CHILDREN!

WHAT ARE YOU SAYING?

DEANNA... WILL YOU MARRY ME?

IT'S NOT A VERY BIG STONE AND IT'S NOT COMPLETELY PAID FOR...

THEY SAID IF YOU WANTED TO EX-CHANGE IT, IT WOULD BE OK...

MICHAEL, I...

I KNOW I'M PUTTING YOU ON THE SPOT BUT... THIS IS THE BEGINNING OF THE YEAR 2000, DEANNA...

AND I THOUGHT IT WOULD BE THE MOST INCREDIBLE THING IF...

MICHAEL—

I SAID **YES!**

KNOW WHAT, GRAMPA? MAYBE IN THE NEW MILLENNIUM WE'LL HAVE ROBOTS THAT MAKE TEA!

WHY? — YOU'VE ALREADY GOT ONE!

THERE'S GONNA BE LOTS OF CHANGES IN THE NEXT 1,000 YEARS, HUH, GRAMPA?

I GUESS THERE WILL BE.

I HOPE WE HAVE REAL 3-D TV SHOWS ...AN' CARS THAT FLY!

MAYBE WE'LL BE ABLE TO GO TO OUTER SPACE— OR EVEN TIME TRAVEL!

THERE WILL BE SOME AMAZING TECHNOLOGY.

I HOPE WE'LL BE ABLE TO SAVE THE WHALES AN' CHANGE THE WEATHER WHENEVER WE WANT— SO EVERY HOLIDAY WOULD BE ON A SUNNY DAY!

WHAT DO YOU HOPE WILL CHANGE IN THE NEW MILLENNIUM, GRAMPA?

PEOPLE.

REFUGEES WAIT IN FREEZING WEATHER

GUERRILLA FORCES OPEN FIRE

VIOLENCE STARTED BY RACIST REMARKS

POVERTY

ENGAGED!! THAT'S WONDERFUL, SON. CONGRATULATIONS!

DEANNA, I'M SO GLAD YOU'RE GOING TO BE PART OF OUR FAMILY!

YOU'RE NOT UPSET, MOM? I KNOW YOU WANTED US TO WAIT.

HONEY, I WANTED YOU TO EXPERIENCE LIFE A LITTLE, FIRST.

BUT, IF YOU'RE SURE, IF YOU'VE REALLY THOUGHT IT THROUGH, IF YOU'RE READY TO MAKE A COMMITMENT THAT WILL AFFECT THE REST OF YOUR LIVES...

WOW, MOM—YOU MAKE THIS SOUND SO SERIOUS!

I'M GOING TO BE A MOTHER-IN-LAW, JOHN.

ELLY...

MIKE AND DEANNA HAVE JUST MADE AN OFFICIAL STATEMENT. THAT'S ALL.

IT COULD TAKE A COUPLE OF YEARS BEFORE THEY DECIDE WHEN AND WHERE THE WEDDING WILL TAKE PLACE!

THEY'RE NOT RUSHING INTO ANYTHING, SO STOP WORRYING ABOUT THEM.

OK. YOU'RE RIGHT. I'LL STOP WORRYING ABOUT THEM.

WHAT IN THE WORLD WILL I WEAR?!!

THAT'S AN AWESOME RING, DEANNA. I CAN'T BELIEVE MY BROTHER ACTUALLY CHOSE IT!

PRETTY, ISN'T IT?

CAN I TRY IT ON?

SURE. WHY NOT?!

MICHAEL, ELIZABETH IS TRYING ON DEANNA'S ENGAGEMENT RING. THAT'S NOT BAD LUCK, IS IT?

I DON'T THINK SO, APRIL... UNLESS...

MMHHH!!!

I CAN'T GET YOUR RING OFF, IT IS TOTALLY STUCK!!

PUT SOME SOAP ON IT!

RIGHT, YEAH. GOOD IDEA! I CAN FEEL IT COMING LOO...

CLINKL!

MOM! MOM! LIZ JUST LOST DEANNA'S ENGAGEMENT RING DOWN THE BATHROOM SINK!!

FEEL ANYTHING, MICHAEL?

JUST THE NEED TO DISMEMBER YOU.

WHAT'S GOING ON?

MIKE'S TRYING TO GET DEANNA'S RING OUT OF THE SINK!

ALL YOU HAVE TO DO IS GET A WRENCH AND UNDO THE "P" TRAP!

I KNOW...

BUT GRANDPA- I CAN SEE IT! IT'S RIGHT THERE! I'VE ALMOST HOOKED IT A COUPLE OF TIMES!

OK

FAR BE IT FROM ME TO TELL A MAN WITH A ROD THERE'S A BETTER WAY TO FISH!!

THEY GOT IT, DEANNA! THEY GOT YOUR RING OUT OF THE SINK!

GLASS XMAS BALLS   FRAGILE

CHRISTMAS ORNAMENTS

THERE SHE IS! WE'LL JUST WIPE 'ER OFF A BIT HERE...

NOW, LET'S SEE YOU PUT IT ON HER HAND JUST THE WAY YOU DID ON NEW YEAR'S EVE!

DON'T LOSE 'ER AGAIN, SON.

I WON'T, GRANDPA, NOT A CHANCE!

... NOT A CHANCE IN THE WORLD.

DEANNA, YOUR HANDS ARE FREEZING! WHY WEREN'T YOU WEARING GLOVES?!!

I WANTED TO SHOW OFF MY ENGAGEMENT RING!!

DO YOU HAFTA GO BACK TO SCHOOL ALREADY, LIZ?

UH-HUH... HOLIDAY'S OVER!

EVERY-BODY'S LEAVING!!!

WHEN DO YOU HAFTA GO, GRAMPA?

WELL... I HAVE A RETURN TICKET TO VANCOUVER, BUT IF IT'S OK WITH EVERYONE, I MIGHT STAY A LITTLE LONGER.

OF COURSE, DAD, HOW LONG CAN YOU STAY?

I'M NOT SURE. ...ONE WEEK, TWO... I WAS HOPING YOU WOULD TELL ME.

HOW ABOUT FOREVER?!

YOU KNOW YOU CAN MOVE IN WITH US IF YOU WANT TO, DAD.

ELLY, YOU DON'T NEED AN OLD MAN LIVING HERE.

AND I HAVE A DOG NOW.

YOU'RE BOTH WELCOME TO STAY. WE HAVE ROOM.

YOU'RE THINKING ABOUT IT, AREN'T YOU.

I COULDN'T DEAR. I REALLY COULDN'T.

BUT IT DOES GET AWFULLY LONELY BACK HOME...

I DID IT, JOHN, I ASKED MY DAD TO COME AND LIVE WITH US—AND HE SAID "YES."

THAT'S FINE WITH ME, EL.

WE'VE TALKED ABOUT THIS MANY TIMES. AND I THINK IT'S A GOOD IDEA. WE ALL GET ALONG—AND APRIL LOVES HER GRANDPA!

WE'LL HAVE SOME ADJUSTMENTS TO MAKE, OF COURSE. WE'LL HAVE OUR UPS AND DOWNS...

I THOUGHT HE SHOULD HAVE OUR ROOM.

THAT IS A "DOWN".

Panel 1: IF MY DAD MOVES INTO OUR ROOM, HE'LL HAVE SPACE FOR HIS DESK AND HIS FAVORITE CHAIR. HE'LL HAVE A BIG CLOSET, A PRIVATE BATHROOM, A BALCONY...

Panel 2: AND WE CAN MOVE BACK INTO OUR OLD BEDROOM UPSTAIRS.

YES. IT MAKES SENSE, ALL RIGHT.

Panel 3: I DON'T WANT TO GIVE UP THIS ROOM, ELLY.

NEITHER DO I... BUT IT'S THE RIGHT THING TO DO.

Panel 4: WHY ARE THE "RIGHT THINGS TO DO" OFTEN THE HARDEST THINGS TO DO?

Panel 5: NONSENSE. I CAN'T PUT YOU OUT OF YOUR ROOM!

Panel 6: DAD, IT'S PERFECT FOR YOU!

WE'LL PUT STAIRS DOWN FROM THE BALCONY SO YOU'LL HAVE YOUR OWN ENTRANCE!

Panel 7: LISTEN, KIDS... I DON'T WANT TO COMPLICATE YOUR LIVES. I DON'T WANT TO BE A BURDEN. AND I DON'T WANT YOU TO DO ANYTHING YOU'LL REGRET LATER.

Panel 9: BUT IF YOU'RE SURE ABOUT THIS — I'M DELIGHTED!!

Panel 10: HONEST, GRAMPA? YOU'RE REALLY COMING TO LIVE WITH US?!

YES, BUT I'LL HAVE TO SELL MY LITTLE HOUSE, FIRST.

Panel 11: OH, MY... NOW THAT I THINK ABOUT IT, THIS IS AN AWFULLY BIG DECISION. I'LL HAVE TO GET RID OF SOME THINGS!

Panel 12: BUT WHEN YOU'RE MY AGE, THAT'S WHAT YOU DO, APRIL. YOU GIVE UP THINGS THAT AREN'T SO IMPORTANT ANYMORE.

Panel 13: ALL I REALLY NEED TO HAVE WITH ME ARE A FEW SPECIAL TREASURES.

Panel 14: ...AND YOU'RE ONE OF THEM.

I'M GOING DOWN TO THE PUB, LIZ—YOU COMING?

I CAN'T. I HAVE TOO MUCH TO DO.

MAN, YOU'RE TURNING INTO A POTTED PLANT!

CANDACE, YOU GET BETTER MARKS THAN I DO. YOU CAN AFFORD TO TAKE TIME OFF!

I'M NOT TAKING TIME OFF. I'VE GOT BOOKS, SEE?—I JUST NEED A MORE STIMULATING ENVIRONMENT.

SOMEHOW, THIS DOESN'T STIMULATE ME TO STUDY.

I DON'T UNDERSTAND IT. I WORK TWICE AS HARD AS CANDACE DOES AND SHE GETS BETTER MARKS!

I GO OVER MY NOTES EVERY NIGHT. I SPEND HOURS IN THE LIBRARY. SHE HARDLY STUDIES AT ALL—BUT SHE PULLS IN 90%!

IT'S LIKE SHE JUST INSERTS SOME KIND OF CHIP INTO HER HEAD AND **BAM!** SHE KNOWS EVERYTHING!

WANT SOME?... THEY'RE CHEDDAR.

I KNOW HOW YOU FEEL, ELIZABETH. SOME PEOPLE MEMORIZE STUFF MORE EASILY THAN OTHERS.

HOW DO THEY DO IT? I WISH I KNEW!—I STRUGGLED FOR EVERY MARK I GOT IN UNIVERSITY.

...SOME OF US JUST HAVE TO SLUG IT OUT.

BUT IF YOU WANT SOMETHING BADLY ENOUGH, YOU FOCUS...YOU FIGURE OUT HOW TO DO IT...

AND EVENTUALLY YOU'LL PULL IT OFF!

BOY, TALKING TO ELIZABETH TAKES ME BACK! — I'D FORGOTTEN HOW HARD IT WAS TO GET THROUGH FIRST YEAR UNIVERSITY!

I'M GLAD SHE TALKS TO YOU, JOHN.

YEAH. I MUST HAVE SPENT AN HOUR WITH HER ON THE PHONE JUST NOW.

IT'S TOO BAD SHE'S SO FAR AWAY.

I DON'T KNOW, EL... SOMEHOW IT FEELS LIKE WE'VE NEVER BEEN CLOSER!

MOM, ARE YOU MAKING PEANUT BUTTER COOKIES?!

UH HUH!

GRAMPA? GRAMPA! MOM'S MAKING PEANUT BUTTER COOKIES!!!

TELL HIM THEY'LL BE READY IN ABOUT 15 MINUTES.

OK!

... I LIKE TO GIVE HIM ENOUGH TIME TO FIND HIS TEETH.

I PUT A LITTLE BOX ON THE BUS FOR ELIZABETH THIS MORNING, JOHN.

OH? WHAT WAS IN IT?

PHOTOGRAPHS, NEW PENS, A LETTER FROM GRANDPA, SOME OF APRIL'S DRAWINGS, SOME HOMEMADE COOKIES, NEW MITTENS, A LITTLE MONEY...

SOUNDS LIKE A LOT OF THOUGHT WENT INTO IT!

I WANTED TO CHEER HER UP BY SENDING SOME SPECIAL LITTLE THINGS FROM HOME.

RRINGG!

MOM? I GOT THE PACKAGE! **WOW!!!** — THANKS FOR THE **CASH!**

113

JOHN, WHAT ARE YOU DOING?

GETTING RID OF THESE PLASTIC CONTAINERS.

BUT... LOOK! THERE'S NO ROOM IN THIS CUPBOARD!

IT'S TIME WE GOT RID OF ALL THE JUNK WE'VE BEEN COLLECTING, EL.

I GUESS YOU'RE RIGHT.

ARE YOU REALLY GOING TO TOSS OUT THESE BOTTLES?

MAYBE NOT. THEY'D BE GOOD FOR NAILS.

WHAT ABOUT THESE? THEY HAVE TIGHT-FITTING LIDS.

SAVE 'EM.

THIS IS A GOOD PACK-ING BOX!

YEAH... AND THIS BIG TIN CAN MAY COME IN HANDY.

I COULD USE THESE FOR WRAPPING GIFTS OR SOME-THING.

SNIFF?

I THOUGHT YOU WERE GONNA RECYCLE ALL THESE THINGS, DADDY.

WE DID...

THEY WERE RECYCLED FROM ONE PART OF THE HOUSE TO ANOTHER.

CBJ 386

114

IT'S HERE, MIKE! THE STORY WE DID ON THE O'CONNOR FAMILY IN IRELAND!

THEY SENT US AN ADVANCE COPY.

ELEVEN PAGES, WEED — AND YOUR PHOTOGRAPHY IS SUPERB.

THE WHOLE THING IS A WORK OF ART, MAN! **THIS** IS WHAT WE'VE BEEN WAITING FOR!!!

SPEAKING OF WAITING, GENTLEMEN... I'VE COME FOR THE RENT.

WE GAVE YOU A BUNCH OF POST-DATED CHEQUES, MRS. DINGLE.

YOU GAVE ME 6. I'M HERE FER NUMBER 7

LOOK! OUR ARTICLE CAME OUT. IT MADE THE COVER OF PORTRAIT MAGAZINE!

WILL IT PAY THE RENT?

I THINK WE CAN SCRAPE TOGETHER PART OF IT.

GOOD.

THEN YOU CAN COME DOWNSTAIRS AND SCRAPE UP THE REST.

SCRAPE SCRAPE

SCRAPE

THIS ARTICLE ISN'T HALF BAD, BOYS!

IT'S THE BEST WORK WE'VE EVER DONE, MRS. D.

THEY'VE TALKED ABOUT MAKING A BOOK OF WEED'S PHOTOGRAPHS!

AND YOUR WRITING, MIKE. ONE GOES WITH THE OTHER.

IT'S ALL JUST TALK RIGHT NOW, BUT IF ALL GOES WELL— OUR WORK IS REALLY GONNA TAKE OFF!

AND THEN, SO WILL YOU, I SUPPOSE.

WE'LL HAVE TO LEAVE LONDON SOON, MRS. DINGLE. THERE'S MORE WORK IN TORONTO.

AND WE BOTH NEED MORE SPACE.

WELL, I CAN'T SAY I'M SURPRISED. I'VE BEEN EXPECTING IT... I'LL MISS YOU.

YOU WILL? REALLY?

YEP...

...OF ALL THE TENANTS I'VE 'AD TO PUT UP WITH—I'VE DISLIKED YOU THE LEAST.

IT'S GONNA BE WEIRD LEAVING THIS HOUSE, WEED.

I DUNNO, MIKE. LATELY, IT'S NOT BEEN MY HOVEL OF CHOICE.

I'VE GOT A LEAD ON A STUDIO IN TORONTO NEAR KING STREET.

THERE'S AN APARTMENT I CAN HAVE ON YONGE.

THE PROBLEM IS—CAN WE AFFORD TO LEAVE? MRS. DINGLE HAS LET US PAY OUR RENT IN INSTALLMENTS—EVEN LET US "WORK IT OFF!" WHEN WE WERE STRAPPED!

YEAH...

SHE'S ALWAYS BEEN SO FLEXIBLE.

I HAVE A DOCTOR'S APPOINTMENT, APRIL—AND I DON'T WANT YOU TO BE LEFT ALONE. WHERE'S GRANDPA?

HE'S WALKING THE DOGS.

BOTH OF THEM?

UH-HUH. HE SAID HE WANTED TO GO OUT FOR A BIT AN' STRETCH HIS LEGS.

YOU HAVEN'T BEEN TO SEE US FOR QUITE A WHILE, ELLY. I'D LIKE TO BOOK YOU FOR A FULL PHYSICAL.

YOU SHOULD DEFINITELY HAVE A MAMMOGRAM, AND CONSIDERING YOUR FAMILY HISTORY, WE SHOULD SCOPE YOUR BOWEL.

WHAT?!

HERE'S A SLIP FOR RADIOLOGY, MAMMOGRAPHY AND THE BLOOD LAB. YOUR PHYSICAL IS BOOKED FOR NEXT WEEK.

HAVE A NICE DAY!

SO, DID YOUR DOCTOR PRE-SCRIBE ANYTHING FOR MENOPAUSE?

HE GAVE ME SOME PILLS TO TRY OUT.

AND HE'S ORDERED A MAMMOGRAM, COLON-OSCOPY AND COMPLETE PHYSICAL.

WOW!

COMPLETE PHYSICAL! YES SIR, DURING THE WAR, THEY LINED US UP, STRIPPED TO THE KNICKERS, THEN POKED AND PRODDED US FROM STEM TO STERN WITHOUT SO MUCH AS A "DO YOU MIND"...

AFTER ALL THAT, THEY HAD THE AUDACITY TO CALL US "PRIVATES".

121

WHY ARE WE ALL SO EMBARRASSED TO BE SEEN BY A DOCTOR? DOCTORS EXAMINE DOZENS OF PEOPLE EVERY DAY!

ONE BODY IS THE SAME AS ANOTHER. WE ALL HAVE THE SAME GENERAL FLOORPLAN.

IF ONLY THERE WAS A WAY TO KEEP US ALL FROM BEING SO SELF CONSCIOUS!

THE DISGUISE GUYS
COSTUME SALES AND RENTALS
SALE ON GOOFY GLASSES

...NAH...
SALES

JUST PUT YOUR CLOTHING IN THIS CUPBOARD, MRS. PATTERSON.
OK.

HERE'S A COVERING FOR YOU. MAKE YOURSELF COMFORTABLE AND THE DOCTOR WILL BE IN TO SEE YOU MOMENTARILY.

I WANT YOU TO KNOW THAT IN AN EFFORT TO PRESERVE MY DIGNITY AND ASSERT MY INDIVIDUALITY...
...I'VE LEFT ON MY SOCKS.

WELL, WHAT DID YOUR DOCTOR SAY?
SO FAR, SO GOOD. I STILL HAVE A COUPLE OF PROCEDURES TO GO THROUGH.

YES, WE'RE GETTING TO BE LIKE A COUPLE OF OLD CARS, EL. A LITTLE RUST HERE, SOME WORN BOLTS THERE, A LITTLE RATTLING UNDER THE HOOD...

BUT AS LONG AS YOU TAKE CARE OF 'ER... SHE SHOULD RUN FOR A LONG TIME!

I DON'T KNOW THAT I LIKE BEING COMPARED TO AN OLD CAR, JOHN!

JUST THINK OF YOURSELF AS A "CLASSIC".

WHY ARE YOU TAKING PICTURES OF GRANDMA OUT OF THE PHOTO ALBUMS, MOM?

IT'S VALENTINE'S DAY TOMORROW, APRIL— SO I THOUGHT I'D MAKE A NICE DINNER FOR US AND YOUR GRANDPA.

AND I WANTED TO PUT SOME OF OUR FAVORITE PICTURES OF HER IN THE DINING ROOM.

WON'T THAT MAKE HIM SAD?

A LITTLE, MAYBE.

BUT JUST BECAUSE SOMEONE'S GONE DOESN'T MEAN THAT YOU STOP LOVING OR REMEMBERING THEM ON SPECIAL OCCASIONS.

AND WHEN WE LOOK AT THEIR PHOTOGRAPHS, WE GIVE THEM A HUG WITH OUR HEARTS...

...BECAUSE WE CAN'T GIVE THEM A HUG FOR REAL!

123

HAVE YOU HAD A MAMMOGRAM BEFORE, MRS. PATTERSON?

NO, BUT I'VE READ ABOUT THEM.

AND YOU DO A REGULAR SELF-EXAMINATION?

I ...TRY TO.

HAVE YOU EXPERIENCED ANY DISCOMFORT? HAVE YOU NOTICED ANY CHANGE? ANYTHING UNUSUAL?

UM...

THEY ARE LOWER THAN THEY USED TO BE.

JUST REMOVE YOUR UPPER CLOTHING AND PUT ON THIS SMOCK. WE'LL BE WITH YOU IN A MOMENT.

SO, WHAT HAPPENS WHEN YOU HAVE A MAMMOGRAM?

IT'S JUST AN X-RAY, REALLY.

IS IT PAINFUL?

THERE'S A LITTLE DISCOMFORT PERHAPS— BUT THINK ABOUT YOUR PEACE OF MIND!

MY MIND ISN'T EXACTLY THE PIECE I'M THINKING ABOUT.

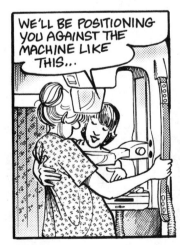

WE'LL BE POSITIONING YOU AGAINST THE MACHINE LIKE THIS...

THE TRANSPARENT PORTION HERE WILL COME DOWN AND COMPRESS YOUR BREAST, ALLOWING US TO GET A CLEAR AND ACCURATE PICTURE OF WHAT'S INSIDE.

ARE WE READY?

HOW FLAT ARE YOU GOING TO SQUASH IT?

THERE. WE'RE DONE!—YOU WERE NERVOUS FOR NOTHING!

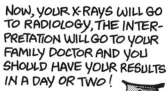

NOW, YOUR X-RAYS WILL GO TO RADIOLOGY, THE INTERPRETATION WILL GO TO YOUR FAMILY DOCTOR AND YOU SHOULD HAVE YOUR RESULTS IN A DAY OR TWO!

A DAY OR TWO?

YES!—ISN'T MODERN TECHNOLOGY INCREDIBLE?!!

YOU CAN'T TELL IF I'M HEALTHY **NOW**?

Lynn

WHERE'S MOM, GRAMPA?

AFTER WORK, SHE WENT TO THE HOSPITAL TO HAVE A FEW TESTS,

WHAT KIND OF TESTS?

HEALTHY PEOPLE TESTS. YOU HAVE THEM WHEN YOU'RE OLDER.

HEALTHY PEOPLE TESTS?

YES!—PEOPLE YOUR MOM AND DAD'S AGE—AND MINE, HAVE THEM EVERY YEAR OR SO!

AND THEY'RE VERY IMPORTANT!

HELLOOOO... I'M HOME!

WELL, I DIDN'T SEE YOU STUDYING—SO I HOPE YOU PASSED!

Lynn

IT'S ALL DONE, CONNIE. I'VE HAD A COMPLETE PHYSICAL—BLOOD TEST, STRESS TEST...

I'VE HAD MY GUTS PROBED, MY LUNGS CHECKED AND A MAMMOGRAM.

AND?

I'M HEALTHY.

THAT'S GREAT!

IT'S A RELIEF, ISN'T IT?

IT SURE IS.

I DON'T HAVE TO GO THROUGH THAT AGAIN FOR ANOTHER TWO YEARS.

Lynn

KEEP, TOSS, KEEP KEEP... TOSS

IT'S GREAT TO BE MOVING, BUT THE DOWNSIDE IS GOING THROUGH ALL THE JUNK YOU'VE COLLECTED!

WE'VE PUT ALL THE STUFF WE DON'T WANT OUT HERE, MRS. DINGLE. WE'LL HAUL IT TO THE DUMP TOMORROW.

KEEP, TOSS, KEEP, TOSS.

WHEN AM I GOING TO MEET MY NEW RENTERS?

TOMORROW.-YOU'RE GONNA LIKE THESE GUYS, MRS. DINGLE.

ANTHONY IS ONE OF MY SISTER'S FRIENDS. I DON'T KNOW HIS ROOMMATE — BUT THEY'LL BE OK!

YOU'RE SURE, NOW.

I WON'T PUT UP WITH RIFF-RAFF!

DON'T WORRY. THEY'RE DECENT, HARD-WORKING KIDS WHO PAY THEIR RENT ON TIME.

REALLY.

THEN I'LL BE MOVIN' **UP** A NOTCH!

HI, MRS. DINGLE! I'M ANTHONY CAINE — AND THIS IS MY ROOM-MATE.

I'M GLENN DENNIS. MIKE HAS TOLD US ALL ABOUT YOU.

I'M SURE HE HAS.

IS IT OK IF WE LOOK AROUND?

YES, BUT YOU'RE NOT TO GO INTO THE DOWN-STAIRS.

THAT'S MY HOME, AN' I LIKE MY PRIVACY.

WE UNDERSTAND. WOULD YOU LIKE OUR RENT CHEQUE NOW?

NO...

I'LL TAKE IT IN MY KITCHEN. I'VE MADE YOU SOME TEA.

MRS. D. SEEMS TO LIKE HER NEW RENTERS!

LUCKY FOR THEM!

OK, WE GOTTA CLEAR OUT THE KITCHEN, MIKE—AND I HAVE A SERIOUS CONCERN. ...WHO GETS "NED"?

I DO!

I BOUGHT HIM.

THOK!

YES, BUT IT IS I WHO HAVE DUSTED AND CARED FOR HIM... WHILE YOU HAVE IGNORED HIM TOTALLY.

HE'S MORE THAN A RUBBER NAKED GUY THAT YOU BOUGHT AT A FLEA MARKET, MIKE. NED REPRESENTS "THE FUTILITY OF MAN."

IN OTHER WORDS... HE IS A FUTILITY SYMBOL.

I DON'T KNOW IF I CAN PART WITH NED, WEEDER. —HE'S LIKE ... FAMILY.

BUT I APPRECIATE HIM MORE THAN YOU DO!

BESIDES, YOU HAVE THE "FICKLE FINGER."

THIS WAS MY DAD'S. IT HAS SENTIMENTAL VALUE!

WHAT ARE YOU TWO ON ABOUT?!

WE'RE MOVING... AND WE BOTH WANT "NED"!

THAT'S THE TROUBLE WITH SEPARATION, ISN'T IT— THERE'S ALWAYS AN INNOCENT VICTIM IN THE MIDDLE.

TAKE HIM, WEED ... HE'S YOURS.

ARE YOU SURE, MIKE?— THIS IS A TRUE SACRIFICE!

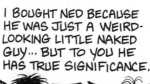

I BOUGHT NED BECAUSE HE WAS JUST A WEIRD-LOOKING LITTLE NAKED GUY... BUT TO YOU HE HAS TRUE SIGNIFICANCE.

INDEED HE DOES.

NED IS "EVERYMAN"... BESIDES, HE'S A COLLECTOR'S ITEM AND SHOULD BE PROPERLY STORED.

REALLY? WHERE ARE YOU GOING TO KEEP HIM?

ON THE WINDOW OF MY CAR!

POINGG!

ELLY... DID YOU JUST THROW A WHOLE BOX OF CHOCOLATES INTO THE TRASH?

YES.

THEY'VE BEEN IN THE CUPBOARD FOR AGES AND NONE OF US NEEDS THE CALORIES OR THE FAT.

BUT THAT WAS A WHOLE UNOPENED BOX!

THINK OF IT AS AN ACT OF WILLPOWER OVER WANT-POWER!

I GUESS YOU'RE RIGHT. WE ABSOLUTELY DO NOT NEED THE CHOCOLATES

POINGG

SAVE ME THE ONES WITH THE CHERRIES.

Lynn

:GROAN: YOU DON'T REALIZE HOW MUCH STUFF YOU HAVE, UNTIL YOU START MOVING!

GOOD THING THIS PLACE CAME FURNISHED.

ARE YOU TWO GOING TO DO ANYTHING FOR MRS. DINGLE? SHE'S BEEN AWFULLY GOOD TO YOU.

WE THOUGHT WE'D TAKE HER DOWN TO THE "BUNG AND WATTLE" FOR LIVER AND ONIONS, AND A GAME OF DARTS!

OH, COME ON! TAKE HER SOMEWHERE SHE HAS TO DRESS UP FOR!!

WE ARE!

YOU WANT TO TAKE ME TO DINNER AT WORTHINGTON'S?!! BUT THAT'S HIGH SOCIETY, BOYS! THAT'S THE RITZ!

IT WAS DEANNA'S IDEA.

WELL, I DON'T KNOW, REALLY.

COME ON. IT'LL BE FUN JUST THE FOUR OF US!

YOU REALLY WANT TO TAKE ME TO WORTHINGTON'S?

MRS. DINGLE, WE WANT TO SHOW YOU HOW MUCH WE APPRECIATE YOU!

WE WANTED TO DO SOMETHING PERSONAL AND, WELL... SENTIMENTAL.

OR... WE COULD JUST HAND YOU THE CASH.

I'M NOT USED TO GETTIN' ALL GUSSIED UP LIKE THIS.

MRS. DINGLE! YOU LOOK GREAT!

YOU THINK SO? I WENT TO THE BEAUTY SALOON AN' EVEN BOUGHT MESELF NEW FOOTWEAR!

THIS IS A SPECIAL NIGHT! NOBODY'S EVER TAKEN ME TO WORTHINGTON'S FOR DINNER BEFORE!

IT'S A PARTY, MRS.D!

I KNOW...

... I JUST WISH IT WASN'T A "FAREWELL".

WHAT A FANCY WAY TO DINE! THAT WAS A LOVELY SUPPER, BOYS. I APPRECIATE THE THOUGHT.

NOW, WHAT'S THIS?

IT'S AN ARTICLE I WROTE ABOUT YOU...AND IT'S GOING TO BE PRINTED IN THE FREE PRESS, WITH YOUR PERMISSION.

AND I TOOK THIS PHOTO OF YOU WHILE YOU WERE WORKING IN YOUR GARDEN LAST SUMMER. WE'D LIKE TO PUT IT WITH THE STORY.

SNIFF...AN' I'M IN A PLACE WHERE YOU CAN'T BLOW YOUR BEAK ON THE NAPKINS!

SO ALL THOSE TIMES YOU SAT AN' ASKED ME QUESTIONS, YOU WERE WRITING A STORY?

DO YOU LIKE IT?

I GUESS IT'S THE TRUTH, ISN'T IT. I 'AVEN'T HAD AN EASY LIFE. NOTHIN'S BEEN HANDED TO ME.

IT'S A GREAT STORY, MICHAEL.

IS THERE ANYTHING YOU'D LIKE US TO ADD OR TO CHANGE?

WELL...

YOU COULD TOUCH UP THE PHOTO AND USE THE WORD "SINGLE" MORE OFTEN.

'NIGHT, MRS. D!

GOOD NIGHT, MR. WEEDER. IT WAS A FINE EVENING!

MRS. DINGLE...WHAT ABOUT THE STORY?

YOU CAN GO AHEAD AND PRINT IT, MICHAEL.

I NEVER THOUGHT MY LIFE HAD MUCH SIGNIFICANCE, BUT THIS IS A GOOD STORY. YOU'VE TOUCHED ME. NOBODY'S EVER GIVEN ME A GIFT QUITE LIKE THIS.

AND IT IS A GIFT, YOU KNOW. YOU HAVE A TALENT THAT'S GOING TO TAKE YOU A LONG, LONG WAY.

THANK YOU.

...DON'T FORGET TO WRITE!

SO ARE YOU GUYS ALL MOVED OUT?

THE PLACE IS YOURS, ANTHONY!

IT'S HARD SAYING GOOD-BYE TO A HOUSE YOU'VE LIVED IN FOR SO LONG.

YEAH...

EVEN THOUGH YOU'VE EMPTIED EVERY ROOM...YOU STILL FEEL AS THOUGH YOU'VE LEFT SOMETHING BEHIND.

Kitchen

SO THIS IS IT. WE'RE OUTTA HERE!

GOOD THING YOU BORROWED A TRAILER!

LONDON CITY LIN

WE'LL UNPACK MY GEAR FIRST, THEN WE'LL HEAD OVER TO YOUR PLACE.

I'LL MISS LIVING WITH YOU, WEED.

IT'S THE END OF AN ERA, MIKE—BUT THE BEGINNING OF A WHOLE NEW WAY OF LIFE.

TRUE.

—FOR THE FIRST TIME IN 24 YEARS... I'LL HAVE A BATHROOM ALL TO MYSELF!!!!

THIS IS IT?

YO! THERE'S STUDIO SPACE ON THE TOP FLOOR.

THE CEILING'S OVER 12' HIGH, MIKE, AN' THERE'S ALREADY SPACE FOR A DARKROOM.

WOW!

SO, WHERE WILL YOU LIVE?

YOU'RE RIGHT, I FORGOT. I'D BETTER LOOK FOR A PLACE.

HOW ABOUT HERE!

...: SIGH :—

I NEVER THOUGHT I'D BE SO HAPPY TO SEE A MESSY ROOM!

COOKING A BIG DINNER TO-NIGHT, EL?

UH-HUH. ELIZABETH IS HERE FOR THE WEEK-END!

IT WAS SO SWEET, CONNIE. SHE CALLED FROM THE UNIVERSITY AND SAID SHE MISSED US SO MUCH... SHE COULDN'T **STAND** IT!!

SHE MISSED MY COOKING, SHE MISSED THE FAMILY AND SHE WANTED TO SLEEP IN HER OWN BED.

SO, SHE GOT ON THE BUS AND DROVE HALF THE NIGHT TO GET HERE!

AND YOU SHOULD HAVE SEEN EDGAR! HE WENT CRAZY WHEN SHE CAME IN THE DOOR!

SHE WENT AROUND HUGGING EVERY-ONE. SHE SAID SHE COULDN'T BELIEVE SHE WAS BACK!!

THAT'S WONDERFUL, EL... WHERE IS SHE?

I DON'T KNOW.

... SHE HASN'T BEEN HOME SINCE SHE GOT HERE!

MICHAEL, THIS IS SUCH A COOL PLACE!

I WAS REALLY LUCKY TO GET IT, LIZ!

IT BELONGS TO A FRIEND OF LAWRENCE'S. HE'S A BOTANIST AND HE'S GOING TO BE AWAY FOR TWO YEARS.

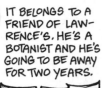

HOW CAN YOU AFFORD TO LIVE HERE?

I'M GETTING AN AMAZING DEAL ON THE RENT.

ALL I HAVE TO DO IS MAINTAIN THE PROPERTY, PAY HIS BILLS, FORWARD HIS MAIL...

AND LOOK AFTER HIS PLANTS.

MICHAEL, IT'S A JUNGLE IN HERE!

YEAH. HE'S GOT EVERYTHING FROM ORCHIDS TO ORANGES.

THIS ROOM HAS THE TROPICALS, THE NEXT IS BONSAI AND EACH ONE COMES WITH A LIST OF INSTRUCTIONS.

WOW.

WELL, AT LEAST THEY'RE JUST PLANTS. IF ONE CROAKS, HE'D NEVER NOTICE.

ON THE CONTRARY...

I'D LIKE YOU TO MEET RUPERT, FLAVIO, BERTRAM, MILDRED, ERNESTINE...

THE GUY WHO OWNS THIS PLACE NAMES HIS PLANTS?

YEAH. SO I HAFTA BE REALLY CAREFUL WITH THEM.

BUT HEY! THIS PLACE HAS CHARACTER—AND IT'S AN EASY BUS RIDE FROM WEED'S STUDIO!

STILL... I DON'T ACTUALLY OWN ANYTHING BUT MY CLOTHES, MY BEDDING, MY LAP-TOP... AND THERE'S NO FOOD IN THE REFRIGERATOR.

AMAZING. MY BROTHER ACTUALLY IS LIVING LIKE A PROFESSIONAL WRITER!

SO, TELL ME ABOUT SCHOOL, SIS...

I DON'T HAVE MY MARKS BACK BUT I THINK I DID OK.

DURING FINALS, I COULDN'T WAIT FOR THE YEAR TO END. I WAS SO TIRED OF CAMPUS FOOD AND CAMPUS LIFE— AND ROOMMATES!

I WAS SO HOMESICK!

WHEN IT WAS OVER, I JUST PACKED ALL MY STUFF AND LEFT. I COULDN'T WAIT TO GET HERE.

AND NOW THAT YOU'RE HOME?

... I MISS SCHOOL!!

IT'S SO WEIRD BEING HOME, MICHAEL. MOM AN' DAD TREAT ME LIKE A KID AGAIN.

THEY ASK ME WHERE I'M GOING, WHO I'M WITH, WHEN I'LL BE BACK—AND I'VE BEEN COMPLETELY INDEPENDENT FOR ALMOST A YEAR!!

THEY HAFTA KNOW THAT STUFF, LIZ—WHAT YOU'RE DOING, WHAT YOU'RE EATING, WHETHER OR NOT YOU'RE BRUSHING YOUR TEETH...

WELL, THEY'RE DRIVING ME NUTS.

THEY'RE PARENTS, SIS...THAT'S THEIR JOB!!!

YOU'RE WORKING?

I START AT MEGAFOOD FULL TIME ON MONDAY.

SO SINCE I HAD A FEW DAYS FREE, I THOUGHT I'D DRIVE INTO THE CITY AND VISIT MY BIG BROTHER!

WELL... IT'S GREAT TO SEE YOU, SIS!

AND LOOK AT US! WE'RE TALKING TO EACH OTHER ADULT TO ADULT. WE CAN BE OPEN! WE CAN BE CANDID—WE CAN BE FRIENDS!

OOF

AAK

OW

LOOK AT THIS! MICHAEL JUST SENT ME HIS FIRST MAJOR ARTICLE— IT TAKES UP HALF THE MAGAZINE!

THAT'S GREAT, EL!

SOME OF HIS ROOMMATE'S PHOTOGRAPHS WERE UP FOR ANOTHER AWARD, AND MIKE HAS BEEN GETTING MORE AND MORE FREE-LANCE JOBS.

OUR SONS ARE DOING WELL, CONNIE. THEY HAVE CAREERS AND GOALS AND PROMISING FUTURES.

YES... IT'S NICE TO KNOW, ISN'T IT.

SO... WHEN DO WE STOP WORRYING?

I ALWAYS WONDERED WHAT IT WOULD BE LIKE TO HAVE KIDS ... AND NOW, I'M TRYING TO IMAGINE MY WORLD WITHOUT THEM!